'Quite brilliant; beautifully, cleverly
observed; funny, heart-breaking.'
Roddy Doyle

'Hopscotch captures the joys, fears and bewilderments
of a 1960s Dublin childhood through the wonderful
prism of an innocent young girl's puzzled attempts to
navigate the muddy waters of her parents' world. It is
written with a deft sleight of hand that makes
it wonderfully funny and moving.'
Dermot Bolger, *Sunday Independent* 'Books of the Year'

'Hilary Fannin carries the reader deep into the
mind of a little girl baffled by the world around
her in her candid, intoxicating memoir . . . a lucid,
crystalline and intoxicating style. *Hopscotch* tells a
private story with candour and exactitude, love and
understanding, artfulness and wit.'
Carlo Gébler, *Irish Times*

'Consistently funny, frequently touching and
full of passages studded with sharp observation,
impressive psychological insight and surreal
invention . . . a small masterpiece.'
Dublin Review of Books

'Brilliantly written and absolutely hilarious. Hilary
is an extraordinary writer and *Hopscotch* is destined
to become a classic of the form.'
Donal Ryan

D0668814

Hilary Fannin

HOPSCOTCH

A Memoir

BLACK SWAN IRELAND

TRANSWORLD IRELAND PUBLISHERS
28 Lower Leeson Street, Dublin 2, Ireland
www.transworldireland.ie

Transworld Ireland is part of the Penguin Random House group of companies
whose addresses can be found at global.penguinrandomhouse.com

Penguin
Random House
UK

First published in the UK and Ireland in 2015 by Doubleday Ireland
an imprint of Transworld Publishers
Black Swan Ireland edition published 2016

This book is a work of non-fiction based on the life, experiences and
recollections of the author. In some cases names have been changed
solely to protect the privacy of others.

Every effort has been made to obtain the necessary permissions with
reference to copyright material. We apologize for any omissions in this
respect and will be pleased to make the appropriate acknowledgements in
any future edition.

A CIP catalogue record for this book
is available from the British Library.

ISBN
9781784161132

Typeset in Goudy by Kestrel Data, Exeter, Devon.
Printed and bound by Clays Ltd, Bungay, Suffolk.

Penguin Random House is committed to a sustainable future for
our business, our readers and our planet. This book is made from
Forest Stewardship Council® certified paper.

MIX
Paper from
responsible sources
FSC® C018179
www.fsc.org

1 3 5 7 9 10 8 6 4 2

For my mother,
Marie Fannin

Contents

1 Baby Mice   9
2 Domestic Circumstance   29
3 Pals   57
4 Bye Bye, Nigel   73
5 Druids and Numbs   100
6 Naked Apes in Polka Dot   137
7 Kneesocked Soldiers of Christ   168
8 My Autobiography   183

Home   218
Acknowledgements   239

Hopscotch (*n.*): A game played by several children or alone, in which players throw a small object into numbered spaces in a pattern of rectangles drawn on the ground and then hop or jump through the spaces in order to reach 'home'.

1

Baby Mice

There's a hole in my bucket, dear Liza, dear Liza,
There's a hole in my bucket, dear Liza, a hole.
Then fix it, dear Henry, dear Henry, dear Henry,
Oh fix it, dear Henry, dear Henry, fix it.

THE SMALL GIRL, STANDING IN FRONT OF THE BLACK-
board, arms akimbo, curly head prettily tilted, mouth
round and pink, clearly enunciating each open vowel and
delicate consonant, is only getting started.

I know this song; I've heard this song before. This is a
song about nothing happening. This is a song about an
empty bucket.

I can't read the singing girl's name badge, but I can see
her blue T-strap sandals. Those are her indoor shoes. I
didn't see her outdoor shoes yet, or her ballet shoes, or her
plimsolls. Those other shoes are hanging in her shoe bag,
in the cloakroom. Just like mine.

With what shall I fix it, dear Liza, dear Liza?
With what shall I fix it, dear Liza, with what?

We listen, seated. Low Babies, we are called. We are in Low Babies. Next year we will be in High Babies. We are small, grey, low-baby mice in roomy grey pullovers. The low-baby boys wear grey flannel shorts, the low-baby girls grey pleated skirts, both gathered over knees bruised from summer. We sit two by two, our indoor shoes neatly held together under the rectangular desks, four small soles, as clean and unsullied as our own, still, unmoved by the music.

Sister Celestine tells us to listen, and we do.

'*Éistígí!*' she says. 'Listen!'

I say 'we' cautiously, because 'we' don't exist yet. We are yet to become a class, a society, one obedient, punishable, entity.

For now, we are a spillage, a collection of four-year-old girls and boys, on the first day of school, whose mothers maybe, but most probably whose fathers (as they are the ones who make the important decisions), have singled us out for a private education. An exclusive education, in the great big red-bricked convent school that sits like a dowager's hat or, in certain lights, a bishop's mitre on top of our brand-new parish.

Some of us, the sharper knives in our midst, those among us who have chosen seats quickly (instead of lingering by the door wondering whether it was safe to cross the sea of parquet flooring, whether we might ever relinquish our grip on the creamy frame and push out into this polished ocean), those of us with a bit of wit and savvy, those of us who already know how to tie our shoelaces and straighten our Alice bands, those of us who dared to stare straight back at Sister Celestine when she asked our name, pen poised in bone-thin finger (rather than look down at the scrubbed wooden desk and walk our small fingers around the open hole for the inkwell), those warriors, those surefooted Indians, who know instinctively to put their hand up before talking, those squaws, those braves, are probably aged five already.

Five. Half of your fingers. Five. At four and four months, I am not one of the advancing posse. I am not yet a sharpened knife.

The shoe bag hanging in the cloakroom, beyond the classroom door, is a worry. What if it's not there at the end of the day? When is the end of the day? How will we recognize it?

In my school bag I have diluted MiWadi orange in a washed-out glass bottle, and in my lunch box two jam sandwiches and two buttered Marietta biscuits. Lunch box: another unwieldy possession. Low Babies have lots of possessions. Lists of necessary accoutrements came in the post, things that we now must recognize and know, things that we own. Our possessions have our names sewn or clearly written on them. My proper name is written on the badge that the nun pinned to my sweater, a name I always fail to recognize as my own. Here I won't be called Billy, my better name. If my name tag said Billy, they'd think I was a boy.

Yesterday we Low Babies owned nothing. Yesterday we just had things. Found and familiar things, friendly things: a hair slide, a kilt pin, a matchbox filled with cotton wool (a bed for the ladybird who died in its sleep), a crocheted hat, two Liquorice Allsorts, a doll's pram with earwigs gathering under the spokes of the red hood.

'Earwigs are drawn to red,' my mother says, eyes on the mirror above her dressing table, rimming her mouth with carmine, in preparation for her walk to the butcher's shop.

'Eahwigs ah dwhan to hed,' she says, the crayon going around and around her open mouth as she watches herself in the mottled glass for any sign of weakness.

Today we Low Babies are stunned by responsibility. We are shellshocked. We have shirts and ties – real ties – and gym slips and pinafores and winter vests and summer vests and pants and kneesocks and long ribbed tights and school bags called *málas*, where we are to keep our copybooks and our sharpened pencils and ink pens with refills and our book of mathematical tables. The book of mathematical tables hisses at me when I lift a corner of its cover. I put it into my new bag slowly, slowly, slowly, so as not to wake up the numbers inside.

And shoes, so many shoes. Shoes with buckles and laces and straps. And a gabardine in winter, and a blazer in spring, and a grey beret, embroidered with the school crest, to be worn regardless of the season.

The boys wear a grey cap.

There are fewer boys than girls in Low Babies. They are a dying breed; we know already that their presence is finite. At the age of six, after first Holy Communion, they will be sent to a different school. At the age of six it will no longer be deemed desirable that we share a classroom.

Everybody knows that the boys have to be shown to the priests before they are seven, so that the priests can look inside and show the world the man.

Anyway, we will be doing knitting, and boys don't knit.

'You have responsibilities,' Sister Celestine tells us, but

I'm not sure if I have. There are none in my pencil case; I hope she won't be cross.

'There are three facts about nuns,' the curly-haired singing girl tells us at little break, spreading her skirt out over her bench and brushing crumbs from her concertinaed pleats.

I squeeze my Marietta biscuits together, make the butter wriggle out of the perforated holes like curious worms.

The singing girl takes a breath, fortifies herself with milk from her Tupperware beaker. She is having a busy morning. There are verses and verses of Liza and Henry to go after break. And now facts as well, nun facts.

'Three important facts,' she says, a little moustache of milk snowcapping her industrious mouth.

The boys stay down the back of the classroom, hands in the pockets of their shorts, eyeing each other like fighters, staking out their territory around the bare nature table. Sister Celestine has gone to the staffroom for her cup of tea. We are marooned. Unsupervised, tears tap on the glass, asking if they can fall.

'Three very important facts. Fact one: nuns are married to God. Fact two: nuns are bald.'

The curly girl is using all her expressions in one go, like Shirley Temple in a candy store. She is too busy with her face to feel frightened. She shakes her head from side to side in astonishment, nods it up and down for maximum veracity, and, once she has drawn all the tiny girl mice into her narrative, folds her dimpled fingers under her sweetheart chin and begins doling out fact three.

'Fact three . . .'

A girl sits beside me, offering a bite of her banana;

her breathing sounds like a faraway train. I decline the banana. The girl is full of objects: pink metal clips hold her blue Alice band in place, two pink bobbins divide her dark-brown hair into short ponytails. Her grey eyes are wide awake but circled with sleeplessness, or maybe with the effort of driving her breath. She looks like a decorative raccoon.

'Fact three: nuns go to bed at eight o'clock and don't get any Christmas presents except a bar of soap and a holy picture. This makes them miserable when they are alive, but when they die they actually get married to God, properly, in heaven, and have wedding dresses and actual hair and lace veils and a tiara, and they really cheer up, and that's called sacrifice. And people who get married on earth are just souls when they die, and they have no bodies and they can't eat, because they have no mouths and they just float around God like clouds.'

'Do nuns have bodies when they're dead?'

My voice sounds like it's hiding under a stone.

'Of course they have bodies. They have wedding dresses and they go to the pictures, they have to have bodies.'

The raccoon girl smiles at me with her moon-ringed eyes, and shrugs her delicate shoulders. I bite into my biscuit.

No one else volunteers to sing, so, after little break, we carry on with Liza's long walk to where she had started from. Precisely nowhere, and with a permanent hole in her bucket.

With what shall I fix it, dear Henry, dear Henry? With what shall I fix it, dear Henry, with what?

*

14

It transpires that responsibilities are things we absolutely have to do. One of our new responsibilities is to hang up our gabardines on the correct hook. My hook has a picture of two yellow fishes on it. I would prefer a picture of a dog, but the dog hook has gone to a boy with a harelip and a famous father.

It is also our responsibility, Sister Celestine tells us, to wear the right shoes, at the right time, on the right day, in the right place.

The long, polished corridors in the convent school, which run between the classrooms and the lunch room, the assembly hall and the convent chapel, are tiled in blue and white and black. We are to walk on the black tiles when we are wearing our outdoor shoes, on the blue tiles when we wear our indoor shoes, and when we are shod in our plimsolls or our ballet shoes the white tiles are our reward.

This is a rule. Fact one: a rule is not for measurement. Fact two: a rule is unbreakable. Fact three: there are more rules than facts.

Another rule is never to speak in the toilet and to always wash your hands carefully and then dry them on the single communal towel.

There must be a pattern to the tiles, or maybe the pattern has to give way to the shape of the polished corridors. Blue tile, black shoe; black tile, blue shoe; white tile, canvas shoe. Walking becomes geometric, squared, rooted. Sometimes the tiles swerve and dissolve, rearrange themselves underfoot to swoop and fall. Sometimes the tiles startle. A sudden blast of the Angelus bells or a loud hymn summoning you to the chapel altar and, flock-like, the tiles take off, landing you in front of an alcove and a plaster saint.

In every alcove, at every turn on those chequered convent streets, a plinth bears a statue. Usually the painted plaster statue is Mary. Mary is the Mother of God. She is also the nuns' Mother, and our Mother.

Even though we have a human mother, Mary is an extra mother, a holy mother, not the same kind of mother as your mother at home in front of the dressing table. The human, lipstick mother cooks fish fingers and draws a beauty spot on her face with her eyebrow pencil and whips off one bulbous earring when she answers the telephone, pressing her ear into the receiver, willing it to spit out the bad news.

Mary, Mother of God, has no make-up, but she does have various aliases. She is variously known as Holy Mary, Hail Mary, and sometimes as the Virgin Mary.

Sister Celestine says that Mary was 'no more than a child' when she was tasked with being the Mother of God. Mary is easily hurt, she says, and that is the main thing about her. Even though she isn't actually alive, she is often hurt by our thoughts and by our deeds.

Mary, whiplashed by selfishness and lies and vanity and talking in the toilets, is bruised if we walk on the wrong tiles, pinched and prodded if our fingers fall from our lips at quiet time.

Poor sore Mary. We are the fruit in her womb.

The Virgin Mary/Holy Mary/Hail-Mary-full-of-grace is often found, on her plinth, holding the baby Jesus in the crook of her arm. The baby Jesus is also just called Jesus, and every now and then Jesus is called the Lamb of God.

Which is a whole other ball game in the deity hierarchy, and remains unexplained by Sister Celestine.

The main thing about Jesus, it seems, besides dying for our sins, curing lepers, turning water into wine and loaves into fishes (loads and loads of loaves into fishes), is that he has a father called Our Father. And Our Father forgives trespasses.

Baby Jesus, sitting there swaddled in the crook of his mother's sculpted elbow, impenetrable and omnipotent as a judge, looks like a small man. An all-knowing, on-top-of-his-game, in-the-driving-seat, ahead-of-the-pack man.

The baby Jesus also has eyebrows on his plaster face, which I want to rub out with my India rubber. Arched, sceptical eyebrows, almost as if the statue artist didn't think that Baby Jesus could take the weight of the world on his small shoulders without them.

Mary, Mary, quite contrary. Holy Mary is an awful worrier, you don't need Sister Celestine to tell you that. Mary, Mary, Mother of God, sighing and weeping and gazing at the ceiling and beseeching and beseeching. And the weight of that plaster baby-man in her child's frail arms, with the weight of the world on the baby-man's shoulders. Tasked with holding him and the world there all night and day and day and night, and where is God when you need him? God, who could have sent a cloud to carry him.

Little break is long over, the song interminable. Henry has just told Liza to fix the bucket with straw.

'Straaaw?' says Raccoon Girl, who has changed places and is now sitting beside me.

'Straaaw?' I say back, because that's what you do when you are friends.

Predictably, the straw is too long to fix the bucket, and has to be cut. But now the knife is blunt, and the stone is dry, and to sharpen the knife the stone must be wet.

'Wehhht?'

'Wehhht?'

I look to the ceiling and beseech God to make the curly-haired girl stop singing about this useless bucket that will leak for all eternity. I don't like Henry, or Liza. I don't like the way they taunt each other with polite questions. Henry and Liza haaate each other, plain as day.

With what shall I? With what shall I? With what shall I?

All the time ignoring the axe. We've all forgotten the axe. Of course.

With an axe, said Henry, said Henry, said Henry.
With an axe, said Henry, said Henry, with an axe.

That puts a stop to their gallop.

But there's still a hole in the bucket. Forever.

Sister Celestine claps. Small hands, brush, brush. We clap. We are 'we' now.

Outside it is September. Yellow. Sea mist and late sun smudged around the edges of the day.

'We will go on our first nature walk tomorrow,' Sister Celestine says. 'Tomorrow we will walk around the convent grounds in our outdoor shoes.'

The girl who sang the endless song might be called

Claudette or maybe Bernadette. Claudette, if that's her name (which would be exciting, because everyone else is called Mary or Siobhan or Margaret, although some people are called Susan, which is a sunny name), has two kittens. Two.

She tells Sister Celestine that when she goes home she's going to put a nylon housecoat on over her brand-new uniform, to protect it from scratches and stains, and clean out the kittens' box. Sister Celestine is impressed with the housecoat; I am impressed with the litter.

Raccoon Girl has a picture of a piglet over her gabardine. Her name is Norhannah, which also isn't Mary.

'My name is Norhannah, but you can call me Norah.'

I tell her my name is Billy, but she has to call me by my written-down name because that is the name on the big school form.

Sister Celestine tells us that God can see us everywhere, and then Mary Harper with the holes in her earlobes asks if he can even see us when we are in the toilet, and Sister Celestine looks terribly disappointed by the question, and whispers: 'Yes, Mary, yes, if you insist.'

On that first day, when I get home from school, I run into the coal shed in our back garden, where even the walls are black with soot, and where bodiless arms sometimes wriggle out between the coal nuggets to drag you down down down. I run in there and shut the door, even though I am more frightened than I've ever been.

'What are you doing?' asks my mother, lighting a cigarette in the back stoop, the tip between her glossy lips, the brown filter ringed with the red imprint of her mouth. 'Ot are ou ooing?'

'Can he see me?' I whisper through the warped wooden coal-shed door. 'Can God see me in here? Can he?'

'Of course he bloody can't,' says my mother, and goes to pick an earwig out of the dahlias.

'Our Father forgives us our trespasses,' I tell my own father, who has a tangerine shirt and a sports jacket with elbow patches.

'Terrific. Do you think he could get the starter to turn over?'

We are late again. My gabardine is letting the fish hook down.

IN 1966, WHICH IS AS NEAR TO THE BEGINNING AS BEGIN- nings ever are, there is the road we live on, a suburban road, long and straight, semi-detached houses sitting two by two along both sides, each two-storey house dressed in identical brick skirts and pebbledashed cardigans, each twosome knitted together at the seams by black guttering.

Between each house a low garden wall separates two identical front gardens, each with mirrored puddles of grass and a tarmacadam pocket on which to park the family car. Each house is accessorized by a flat-roofed garage at its opposite elbow, a practical addition in which to store mousetraps and paraffin and broken things and tins of baked beans and picnic salmon in case the world ends.

There are six of us in my family. My father, with blue

eyes and suede shoes and untipped cigarettes and a waterproof wristwatch that tells him where he is really supposed to be. My mother, with red lipstick and a piano that she stands beside, singing notes and scales. The sounds drift out of her glowing mouth like small fishes trapped in bubbles; the notes float up to the low ceiling and hang there, unheard, until they dry up and fall on to the floor.

Also in my house are my siblings, three of them. Sibling is a difficult word to fully understand. My siblings are each other's brother and sisters. I'm not altogether sure if, or how, they are related to me. They are older than me. As much as a whole decade older. They wear bellbottom jeans and listen to the Beatles.

My siblings amount to two smoky-eyed older sisters, Louise and Anna. Louise is eleven months older than Anna, which makes them fifteen and fourteen. They sleep in twin beds in the same darkened room, and use the telephone a lot, and they iron each other's long wavy hair to make it dead straight.

I also have a boy sibling, my brother, John, who is thirteen months younger than Anna, and who has brown eyes and curly dark hair, and who I frequently meet under the dining-room table for meetings.

My siblings painted the walls inside of the garage limegreen and pink. Sometimes they sit in there, on old car seats and a broken stepladder, to talk in whispers about important things. I am not allowed to join them. Anyway, I really only ever go into the garage to look at the three glass jars of baby beetroot on the garage shelves. They stand next to the remaining tins of Batchelors beans, most of which were eaten when Russia and America stopped shouting at each other about Cuba. (Now they are just muttering under their breath.) The baby beetroots look festive under the stretched fluorescent garage light, purple bauble on purple bauble. You could nearly look forward to Armageddon, John says.

I usually look forward to Christmas, but I'll ask Norah what Armageddon is, and then maybe I can look forward to that too.

I am the youngest. By a long shot. I don't know of what.

I am two things, depending on who you are talking to or who the person talking about you is talking to. Mainly I am 'the Baby', but I am also 'the Mistake'.

Each house on our road has a sheltered porch and a front door featuring a playful fan of bubbled glass, and a knocker like a cheap buckle, and an electric bell and a provocative slit, low down, for the postman, who doesn't have a bad back, yet, to post the tax demands through.

My father collects the post in the mornings, bending down to pick up the brown envelopes, then running his thumb over the dry manila and putting the offending bills in his pocket.

I like our porch. Our porch is a castle and a dungeon and an aeroplane. Our porch is Australia and France and a car. It is a swimming pool and a department store and sometimes, if we are feeling brave, it is a lunatic asylum that Norah and I incarcerate all the lunatics in, and then throw away the key. We run then, fast down to the bottom of our road, so as not to hear the crazy people scream. We run and run, and then I turn to see if Norah is at my back, and see her holding on to a neighbour's pillar, smiling, bent forwards, waving down her breath, asking it to fill her lungs again.

I don't like scary games, I don't like when we people the porch with big imaginings. I like when Norah and I sit on the porch, dressed in bedsheets after a satisfying game of emperors, to discuss Protestants. Norah has heard that they have black marks on their souls, and maybe we should look for those as a test.

The porch, in reality the size of two spread-out handkerchiefs, is also where the woman from the caravans sometimes sits to drink the tea my mother carries out to her, tea from a pastel-coloured teacup on a pastel-coloured saucer.

'Sugar?' my mother enquires, her painted-on eyebrow prettily arching.

'Yes, ma'am,' the woman replies. 'God be good to you.'

God hasn't been particularly good to my mother, but then God has been even worse to the caravan woman, whose face is bruised by sun and fist and wind, and whose mottled legs grow out of ankle-socks that should be worn by a man and shouldn't be worn with broken sling-back sandals.

But we don't know any of that yet. In the beginning, we are unaware of God's plan.

'What's wrong with the caravan woman?' I ask my mother. 'Where is her house? Why does she drink her tea on the porch? Why doesn't she come inside?'

'She doesn't like the inside,' says my mother. 'She lives on the road.'

'Is she drawn to roads?'

*

In the summery autumn of 1966, in that newly built suburb, north of Dublin town, days are dawning fresh as a daisy under a blameless sun. The angel-blue sky, carefully coloured in right up to the edges. Clouds sail by puffy and white, scarred by the occasional jet stream, which causes us children, lying now on our backs in the stubbled grass of our back garden, to look up.

'That aeroplane is from America.' Norah exhales, bees buzzing in her chest. She sits up to cough.

'Maybe it's from Paris,' I reply.

'Paris,' my mother sighs, unpegging her good black slip and my father's tangerine shirt, hanging out Louise and Anna's nylon night-and-day dresses. 'Paris. Christ.'

She lifts the sky-blue plastic washing basket from the dry grass, mounts the three steep steps to the back door, basket on her hip. 'Paris.'

My mother sounds as if the Henry in the Liza-and-Henry song has stepped out of his long dirge to fix the bucket, axe out her insides and fill her full of straw. I watch until even her shadow disappears inside the house.

'Parisians have very complicated underwear,' Norah says, exhaling slowly, catching her breath train. 'And they eat raw mince and feed their little dogs under the table, and then lick their own fingers.'

It's Saturday. My mother is frying bread and eggs and mushrooms and tomatoes and bacon in a pan on the electric cooker. My father is propping up his forehead with his hands, elbows resting on the yellow Formica table.

'I have news,' she says. 'I'm joining the Red Cross Hospital Chorus. I'm going to sing again. It's a wonderful organization, lovely people, singers who want to sing. Sing to the sick. Folk songs. Light opera. Modern classics.'

She flips the egg, breaks into the opening bars of Gilbert and Sullivan's 'Three Little Maids from School', which makes Liza and Henry's sad ballad sound positively groovy. My father winces in slow motion, like the sound hurts.

'I'm hoping to bring a little bit of Judy Collins to the table.'

'Who is Judy Collins?' my father mouths to me.

'She's a singer lady on the radio who turns turns turns. Turns and turns and turns. Turns and turns and turns and turns.'

'Right. Right.' His eyes are pink, the air around him smells like metal.

'We will travel to hospitals and homes the length and breadth of the country to sing to the sick and the clinically insane.'

'Actual lunatics?' I ask.

'Possibly. Although I don't think they're called that any more.'

'That should be a barrel of laughs,' says my father, eyes watering, little nests of spittle forming at the corners of his mouth.

His blue, pink-rimmed eyes close. He fails entirely to notice the fried egg torpedoing from the frying pan, glancing off the Styrofoam ceiling board, hovering like an alien craft above his head. He does not see the two slices of fried bread boomerang around the sunny kitchen, the slivers of airborne back bacon crash-land by his new suede shoes, the fried tomatoes falling heavily like wrinkled missiles, the mushrooms raining bullet-like over the shiny Saturday table.

Outside our forest-green, bubble-glass front door is our newly built road, the gleaming pavement beyond our gate neatly punctuated by evenly planted saplings. Delicate, hopeful little trees, clutching at the sandy dry soil, wondering if this new earth would hold them.

Outside our forest-green, bubble-glass front door, neighbours sweep their porches, wash important cars, walk purposefully up to the newsagent at the top of the road for a packet of Sweet Afton and an inky newspaper. They pop into the grocer's for a bunch of bananas and a tin of mushy peas, visit the long pale butcher in his cold white shop for six pork chops, the tips of their polished shoes pushing into the blood-speckled sawdust that covers his morgue-like floor. They remember, too, to drop into the chemist's shop and pick up a tin of Alka-Seltzer and a packet of barley sweets from the grim, beetroot-coloured pharmacist in his wire-framed glasses, the sweet packet, when he pushes it across the wooden countertop, dwarfed by his great big pharmaceutical fist. They might pause then to nod at his silent wife, captive behind the wooden counter, a mouse-like child by her feet.

Our next-door neighbour has loads of babies. Girl babies. One after the other, baby girls tumbled out of their smiling mother like spongy acrobats. Those babies have no eyebrows, just big solemn eyes. Ensconced in their shared pram, the babies watch, from over the low back-garden wall, my mother peg up the washing. Stilled by the sight of her long red nails snapping open the dry pegs, the girl babies sit unblinking in the pale sun, eyebrow-less spectators, in their bleached, dry-grass back garden.

'Which one is that?' my mother says, a wooden clothes peg between her white teeth, my father's pocket handkerchiefs frothy pennants trying to take off in the breeze.

'Whikoneistaht?'

In the kitchen, my mother, small and perfectly formed, her painted eyebrows and cuticle-creamed fingertips minor players in the orchestra of her beauty, pours out a cup of tea for the caravan woman, who has come knocking on the Saturday door and is sitting now on our gleaming porch, waiting for refreshments, unaware of the breakfast casualties scattered, limb-torn, across the kitchen floor. My mother, carefully avoiding stepping on to the beached egg, places four Marietta biscuits on a lemon-yellow side plate, next to the cup and saucer, pours milk from the bottle into the pale-blue jug, refills the sugar from its paper packet into the pale-pink bowl. Stepping over the sunken tomato missiles, the blunted mushroom bullets, the broken back rashers, she smooths down her Crimplene skirt, pats her back-comb, picks up the neatly set tray and, as she taxis down the narrow hall towards the front porch – where the caravan woman still sits, waiting patiently, biding her time, taking the weight off her bare, broken-veined legs – smilingly acknowledges herself in the sun-shaped hallway mirror, its golden spokes radiating out from its glass orb, her own lovely face at its epicentre, its point of fusion.

'Join me in a cup, ma'am, and I'll read the leaves for you.'

My mother hesitates.

'Sure, what harm could it do you, ma'am, to glance into the future?'

What harm could it do me, thinks my mother, turning on her pretty heel to fetch herself a nice clean cup. Probably no harm at all, because what happens happens, and what doesn't happen doesn't happen, and we're really none the wiser anyway.

2

Domestic Circumstance

WE ARE HIGH BABIES. OLD HANDS. SEASONED MICE. Our outdoor shoes walk us right out the convent gates and down the road as far as the causeway, and on to the strand. We walk two by two, holding hands.

Fact one: there are more than two hundred billion stars in our galaxy.

Fact two: there are more than one hundred billion galaxies in the universe.

Fact three: God is in charge of every single one of those galaxies, and still he chose to send his only son to Earth to save us. Us. Just us.

Sister Celestine says that there are more stars in the sky than there are grains of sand on this cloudy beach.

God made the world in seven days, she says. Jesus was tiny, ladybird-sized, in a matchbox in God's pocket. God sent the Archangel Gabriel to knock on Mary's bedroom window, to tell her that Jesus had moved into her womb, even though she didn't know it yet. Archangel Gabriel said that Mary was doing God a really big favour by being Jesus's Earth mother, and that when she died she would rise up to heaven on a cloud and have eternal life among the angels and saints.

He also said suffering little children would flee unto her. But maybe he told her that later. After Jesus was born.

Fact: donkeys have a cross on their backs, built into their fur. This is because Mary rode on a donkey on her way to the manger to have Jesus. The donkey is a lowly beast, but he is also loyal and faithful, and anyway we can't all be high-fliers.

The cross on the donkey's back is one of the clues God left us, to show his love for us.

Fact: there are lugworms on the strand. They look like they are already dead. The worms are all part of God's plan. God's plan is a mystery. A mystery means something we can't understand, yet. God's plan is also infinite and varied.

A woman drove off the edge of the harbour. Dawn tells me.

We are sitting on the window seat in the snooker room, looking out at the trawlers tied up next to the pier, and at the narrow black channels of oily sea between them.

The men are playing snooker, their pints, dewy and black, lined up in front of the bar hatch and on the tables around the unlit fireplace.

Two of the pints belong to my father. When he finishes them, we will probably drive home.

'Line them up' is what you do when the bar is about to close, when Frank, the barman, is mopping down the counter and saying 'Gentlemen, gentlemen' as if they are late for bed.

There are two Franks the barman, Old Frank and Young Frank. Old Frank gets a little bit cranky and likes you to pay for your round as soon as you get it; Young Frank lets you pay for your round as soon as you can.

Before Young Frank goes home for his lunch, he lines them up on the counter. Sometimes the lined-up drinks last until Frank comes back and opens up the bar again.

When Frank goes home he has his dinner, even though it's the middle of the day, then he has a nap, and then he gets back into his car and drives all the way to the bottom of the pier and opens the big wooden door of the club and comes upstairs to start again.

'What kept you?' the men say.

Dawn and I have smoky bacon crisps to keep us going, and bottles of Mirinda Orange, with straws.

Straaaws. I could say straaaws out loud, but Dawn wouldn't know what I meant. Dawn is my other friend, but she goes to a different school, and she is unhappy there.

Dawn says that the woman who drove her car over the edge of the pier, and into the harbour, was wearing her indoor shoes outdoors. Party shoes. The kind that have long leather thongs attached, that you criss-cross up your legs and tie in a bow under your knees.

Dawn says that the woman had criss-crossed the leather ribbons on her sandals, all the way up her legs, and tied them in a bow under her knee. Dawn says that the thongs must have loosened when she went downstairs and left the bar, or maybe when she was outside on the pier searching in her basket, impatient for her keys.

She tried to swim out of the car window, Dawn says, when the car was filling up with water, but the loose leather thongs wrapped themselves around the pedals and she couldn't get the party shoes off her feet. Dawn doesn't know which pedal, the accelerator or the clutch, or maybe the brake, or maybe all three. Maybe the leather thongs went in, around, up and over all three pedals, like knitting. Like knit one, purl one.

I can't purl. I'm the only one in my class who can't purl. Even though they don't actually do knitting in Dawn's school, she can already cast on and knit and purl and even cast off, which is the most difficult thing to do. It's good that she can knit because they do a lot of sport in Dawn's school, and she doesn't like sport, and anyway they don't ever choose her for the team.

In my school they call me Thumbelina, because I'm small. I don't grow, or cast on, or cast off, or purl.

'Thumbelina?' says Dawn. 'Chance would be a fine thing!'

She is making her eyes wide, to look like a crazy person, and she is eating up her crisps. She grows and grows, even though she doesn't want to. I don't really want her to tell me the rest of the lady-with-the-thongs story, but I also really *do* want her to tell me the rest of the lady-with-the-thongs story. Sometimes Dawn is very sad, sometimes she stops talking in the middle of her sentences and looks out the window instead. Then she remembers that you are her friend and then she starts talking again.

Dawn's dad owns the yacht that my father sails on, and Dawn's mother speaks with an American accent even though she's not American. Sometimes Dawn's mother asks us to hold her hand while she walks downstairs to the ladies' room.

'You kids wanna walk me to the rest room?' she says, and we do. While she is inside, we wait for her outside the door so that we can guide her back up again.

Sometimes she smashes her glass down on the counter-top and says: 'Don't tell me what I can or cannot do.'

'Don't tell me what I caaaan or caaannot do.'

Dawn's dad is called the skipper. My dad is one of the crew. Yachts are called 'she'.

'She's a thirty-four-footer,' says the skipper.

'Bloody nice,' say the crew.

Dawn is ready to talk again. The woman's car filled up with water, she says, and her long hair rose up from the top of her head, and from the nape of her neck, and touched the roof. And her cheeks puffed up with sea water, and her breath roared inside her head, louder than the sound of the ocean when you hold a shell to your ear.

And when the digger came trundling down the harbour, and the boatman shooed all the unknown, curious people out of the way, and while they gathered to watch, even though they were unwelcome, the lady's car was wrenched out of the water.

'Sucked out of the sea with a pop,' Dawn says. 'Like when your thumb is dragged from your mouth.'

We make the pop sounds on the window seat. Pop. Pop.

'The woman was still inside,' Dawn says, 'and her eyes were wide open.'

All part of God's plan.

WE HAVE WALKED OUR HIGH-BABY SELVES RIGHT OUT the convent gates and down the road as far as the causeway, and on to the strand. A caterpillar of grey behind Sister Celestine's narrow blue-black back.

The boys want to dig the lugworms out of the sand with their bare hands, carry them back to school in the pockets of their grey flannel shorts and put them on the crowded nature table. Sister Celestine says we can collect shells instead. The shells are dry and firm and shaped like ice-cream cones.

'If you put them to your ear, you can hear the ocean roar,' says Sister Celestine.

But I know that already and I don't want to think about the ocean roaring in my ears, and my hair floating up from my neck and my legs turning into fish scales, and a mermaid me floating up to the ceiling above my mother's piano.

Sister Celestine says there is a beach in County Cork (which is one of the twenty-six counties in Ireland that the Catholics own, not one of the other six, also in Ireland, that the Protestants own) and that, on the beach, there are special shells which have an image of the Virgin Mary actually imprinted on them. Actually. In real life.

The shells, like the cross on the donkey's back, are more loving clues left by God. Clues that he scattered around after he had finished creating Earth so that we would believe in him and his eternal goodness, and so that we'd remember that he was inside of us guiding our thoughts and our deeds.

The donkey's furry cross, snowflakes (each one entirely individual) and our fingerprints (also utterly unique) are

34

just some of God's loving clues. Some of his finishing touches.

'Utterly unique' and 'entirely individual' are the phrases Norah and I use when we play shop at the end of my back garden. Draping dry-as-a-bone, board-stiff tea towels, freshly unpegged from the washing line, around our waists and over our narrow shoulders, we set up our shop by the hedge and use the lime-green leaves as real money.

Dressed up in our tea-towel finery, we admire each other greatly.

'Madam,' I say to Norah in an important, scratchy voice, 'you look utterly unique and entirely individual.'

'Well, thank you, madam,' says Norah.

'Well' – breath – 'Thank you.' Breath.

Sister Celestine says that you can see Mary's face as clear as day on the imprinted shells on the beach in County Cork. You can see, tattooed on to the shells' delicate surface, the shape of her robe, and her arms held open, beseeching the people of the world to remember their responsibilities.

The shells are the colour of jewels, Sister Celestine says, pink and mauve and silvery blue, and Mary's alabaster face shines out from the centre, and it is the most beautiful face in the world, free from artifice, imbued with suffering and her sad, sad, love for us.

The rain is starting to fall now on the strand. I think maybe Sister Celestine is going to cry, or sing a hymn. Her thin arms are held aloft, reaching up for God's watery sun. Angels' tears fall out of the clouds to decorate her delicate face.

I think Sister Celestine feels very close to God.

Especially close, closer than the other nuns, who are bigger and pinker and tuck into their lunch and blow their noses very loudly into their nicely ironed handkerchiefs.

Sister Celestine's sunward, rain-startled face is so tiny it swivels around inside her wimple, like a long-playing record. We have been on the beach for a long time. I look up at the big wet purple sky, open my mouth, drink in the sanctifying grace.

All the way back along the shore road, our gabardines darkening with autumn rain, Norah and I practise being Shell Mary. We hold hands, allowing our outside arm to fall open, palm facing forward, into the now driving rain. Heads demurely tilted, eyes cast down, we beseech everyone in the world to always draw their margins with a red pen, and not to forget their knitting on a Thursday.

'And their threes,' I remind Norah. 'Make sure they do their threes the right way round.'

My mother tried knitting once, but the wool got tauter and tauter with each angry stitch, until it snapped, and the needles were fired into the kitchen drawer.

She went to the doctor.

'Stop knitting!' said the doctor.

The doctor was a woman with a man's name and a hair bun and wrinkles.

'Stop knitting,' she said, 'and take these.'

The pills are to make my mother sleep, and to stop her worrying about unknitted bed jackets. I have thick yellow plastic needles and scratchy red wool. I am knitting A Scarf. Or, if the scarf is too narrow, A Hairband. I don't like Thursdays. On Thursdays the wool gets tauter and tauter with each in-around-up-and-over, until it snaps.

Sister Celestine doesn't know what to do with me. The Virgin Mary is rolling her eyes towards the ceiling like a crazy person. Another small nick in her plaster armour.

Sometimes, while we are concentrating on our knitting (or our not-knitting), Sister Celestine tells us mice about all the beauty in the universe. Her bony knuckles clutch at the silver cross lying flat on her navy-blue habit, the sleeves of her long black cardigan fall down over her doll-thick wrists, and she tells us about all the mysterious beauty that awaits us when we enter the kingdom of heaven, when we too take our rightful place at God's feet, among the angels and saints.

'All we have to do is remain pure and good and brimful of grace, children, and all God's mysteries will be revealed to us.'

After Sister Celestine reminds us about taking our place at the feet of Jesus, Norah and I put our knitting neatly into our school bags and walk the corridors to the lunch room very very slowly. Whether we are in our indoor shoes, our outdoor shoes, our ballet shoes or our plimsolls, we walk slowly and carefully. We are like the women returning from the well with jars of water on our heads to wash the feet of Jesus. We are not going to spill a single drop of our sanctifying grace; we are going to remain utterly brimful.

'Sooner or later, all God's mysteries will be revealed to us,' I tell my father as we gun down the suburban road on the way to the convent.

'Yeah? You couldn't ask him if he's seen my chequebook anywhere, could you?'

There is a thin line of sweat over my father's lips. His eyes are very busy, trying to figure things out.

I'll say a prayer for his chequebook to Saint Anthony. Anthony is the lost-property saint. Or maybe he's lost causes, I can never remember which one.

Now that we are in High Babies, and allowed to go on nature walks outside the convent gates, we have to do homework. We have to do our homework in the *cistin* while our *mhamaí* make the tea. Those are the homework rules.

A *cistin* is a kitchen in the Irish language, which is a language we don't speak in my house, and a *mhamaí* (which sounds like 'wamee') means mammy in Irish. *Mhamaí* is a word that Norah and I like to say a lot.

'Waaammeee?'

'Waaammeee?'

I'm doing my homework at the yellow Formica-topped kitchen table. I have to remember to write my threes in the right direction. Writing my numbers backwards makes the Virgin Mary wince. I know wincing. My father does a lot of wincing on the weekends when the radio is too loud.

I can't find a rubber to rub out my backward threes. If I scrunch some white sliced bread up in a lump and roll it over my copybook, the threes might get mopped up, rubbed out. My brother showed me how to do it. 'Weird things work sometimes,' he says.

My mother is cooking the tea, which is what people in Ireland call their dinner. She is cooking spaghetti.

38

'Sphagetteeee?' says Norah, because her mother cooks potatoes.

'Sphagetteeee?' I say back, even though I like spaghetti.

My mother is singing a song to the cooker, which makes it hard to concentrate on the moving threes. The song is about castles in the air made of ice-cream. My mother sings the ice-cream song to the cooker as if there are more than four electric rings listening to her.

In the song, the floating ice-cream castles end up being turned into ordinary old clouds, and then those old clouds block the sun and, as well as that, they rain and pour on everyone.

And that's probably not good news. It's actually quite a sad song when you listen to it.

Before she had us, before she was tasked with being our mother, my mother was a singer, with jet-black hair. When she was the singer, with jet-black hair, she got a very big role, a leading role, in a musical comedy that was on in a famous theatre in the city. (That kind of 'role', by the way, is different to the 'rolls' that we get with butter and soup in the convent lunch room. It is also a different kind of roll to the roll that you do downhill when the grass isn't wet.)

The kind of roles my mother had meant that she had costumes delivered to the stage door in a wicker basket, and flowers pinned to her waist, and lots and lots of people clasping their hands together and telling her that she was truly talented and truly, truly beautiful, and that her future was looking exceedingly bright. 'Of that there is no doubt,' they said to her, walking backwards out of her dressing room so as not to miss one split second of her radiance.

None of those things apply to soup or grass rolls.

'Was I good?' my mother asked her mother when she came home later that night, dancing on air, with all her loveliness still inside her, happy because she had triumphed in her first big, important role.

'Was I good? Was I? Was I good?' my mother asked her mother, who had been in the audience that night, quite possibly with a flattened stoat around her shoulders.

'You turned your feet in,' my mother's mother replied.

THE NAME OF THE BEACH IN COUNTY CORK WHERE YOU can find Mary, Mother of God, imprinted on to the shells is the Virgin Mary Bank.

'We should go to the Virgin Mary Bank,' I tell my father.

We are driving fast down the gravelled convent drive. We are late, again. Really late.

'Does she give credit?' he asks, hitting the brake.

He still can't find the ruddy chequebook, and now it's Friday.

'Where is the ruddy chequebook?' he asks. 'Where is it?'

My father's jaw is shaved clean. His hands shake very slightly when he puts his cigarette to his lips. Flick lighter. Sweet Afton. Untipped.

He looks at me. Now he sees me, now that he has stopped trying to figure ruddy things out.

'Who's Daddy's pal?' he asks.

40

'Billy is,' I reply.

'Who's Billy's pal?'

'Daddy is.'

Before he opens the car door I drink in all the great smells of him: smoke, Old Spice, corduroy, old beer hosed down with new toothpaste.

We walk into the cloakroom together hand in hand. We hang my gabardine on my coat hook with the picture of the yellow fishes above it, fishes who now thoroughly dislike presiding over my tardy outerwear. They want to protect a gabardine that gets hooked at ten to nine, not at ten to ten or even, like this morning, at ten to eleven.

He pushes open the door of the classroom. I slip inside, under his elbow-patched arm, seek my desk and Norah's steady, rattle-breath shelter.

'Domestic circumstance,' he smiles to Sister Celestine.

The cigarette, a good old buddy of his, hangs out in his lips; his leather elbow patches, stalwarts, men you can lean on, clasp each strong arm; his blue cravat, a debonair advocate, is exactly the same colour as his eyes.

'Domestic circumstance.'

He never elaborates. He's never asked to.

Sister Celestine, God's bride – chalk-stained, rosary-fingered, a flurry of loose thread and tiny, twitching musculature – smiles at him from behind her desk.

Who can really tell the human from the divine? Who knows who was made flesh?

He has important business to attend to in the advertising industry, he must go away to draw things and kick some ideas around. The door closes. The class resumes its parables: virgins and lepers and prodigal sons. Those are the things we kick around, and jumpy numbers that write themselves backwards, and the Irish for stuff.

Friday is my favourite day of the week, except for Saturday. On Friday I get a can of Apala, which is a fizzy apple drink, and a packet of Hula Hoops and I sit on the red couch and watch *I Love Lucy*. Everybody loves Lucy, no matter how much of a mess she makes of things. Everybody thinks she's as cute as a button (personally, I think she could do with a long bath and an anti-knitting pill). Cute is a tricky word. If you are cute in America it means that you have a pretty little face and evenly spaced teeth and nylons and slingback shoes and quite a lot of bubble baths. If you are cute in Ireland it means that you can get away without buying your round.

I am allowed to go to bed really late on Fridays, later than the serious news on the television, almost as late as the bit at the end, before the television is over for the night, when a holy person tells everybody to switch off the lights and unplug the kettle and say a prayer for all the black babies in Africa and give sixpence to the polio collection outside Mass next Sunday. I can go to bed so late I feel like sand has blown into my eyes. I can climb into bed in the little room over the garage and turn on the radio on my bedside table and listen to *Late Night Extra* and wait and wait and wait and try not to fall asleep until he comes home, smelling of cigarettes and corduroy. And even if I do fall asleep I wake up again when I hear his key in the door. Sometimes my mother comes up the stairs and sits down and says 'Are you not asleep yet?', which, when you think about it, is not the brightest thing to say, because if I was asleep I wouldn't be able to answer her.

'No,' I say, and then I ask her if I can hypnotize her.

I like hypnotizing my mother. It's very easy and very effective. I just take whatever necklace she is wearing off her neck, without disturbing her back-comb, and then I slowly swing it from side to side in front of her face and say 'Look deep into my eyes and sleep, deep into my eyes and feel yourself drift away'. Actually, it's too easy. My mother falls asleep sitting up, like a puppet without her strings, and then you have to wake her up and remind her to go to bed in her own room.

I'm either a very good hypnotist or the don't-worry-about-the-ruddy-knitting pills are making her sleepy.

I stay awake after she goes back down the stairs to wake herself up with a cup of tea, and then I hear his key in the door.

'I'm going up to say goodnight to Billy,' he calls to the stonily closed doors along the hallway and landing. He conquers the stairs, pushes open the half-closed door, sits next to me in the bluey dark. There is a warm smell around him of honey and whiskey, and something else like flowers or chocolate or sun. He must have kicked around some good ideas today.

'Who's Billy's pal?' I ask him. Even though I already know the answer.

Saturdays are the best days. Saturday is reserved for me and him. Saturday has a sold sign on it. My friends know not to knock on the door and ask me out to play on Saturday. Usually on Saturday mornings, while my mother is in the bath preparing for her concert and getting ready to look at both sides of life now, my father and I get into whatever car he is driving, and we go. We just head off.

Mostly, we turn left when we nose out of our estate, put our foot down and drive out to the very end of the coast road, to the harbour, where the sea bashes up against the wall. When we get there, we park where the fishing boats are moored, and where rainbow-coloured oil floats on top of the water. We walk hand in hand, looking into empty fish boxes for guts, looking at the little bits of nylon rope that have been trodden into the ground by the trawler-men's boots. The ropes look like tangled messages, like secret writing, like a language we can't read yet. We walk to the end of the harbour, smelling the salt and diesel and sometimes, depending on which way the wind is blowing, we smell vinegar from the chip shop over the road.

We walk, and we talk about things, about what kind of dog we would have if we had a dog, and what countries we would visit if we had the wherewithal (wherewithal is another word for money). And we don't get frightened by the seagulls, who are marble-eyed and fierce, and who can actually eat cats; the seagulls who sit on top of the fish boxes asking us in seagull language what the hell are we looking at.

'Whaatawwyaalaakanaaat?'

'Nothing,' we say. 'We are looking at absolutely nothing.'

And then we stroll into The Club, like professionals.

Mostly, when we're in The Club and the men are lining them up and playing snooker, Dawn and I sit in the window seat, with our smoky bacon crisps, and have our important conversations. Conversations punctuated by the snooker balls rolling into the clack-clacking nets that hang on the side of the big green table. Yellow, green, brown, blue, pink, and the bluebottle black. Clack, clack, clack, clack, the final splintering sound pretty much always followed by one of the men hopping around in his canvas sailing trousers (even though he's a long way from a deck or a squall), waving his snooker cue above his head and saying: 'Lovely, fucking lovely. Your round, you bastard.'

Dawn and I, hidden in plain sight on our window seat, are invisible, even though we are real, even though we can see each other clear as day.

But this Saturday, my father is going racing in Dawn's father's yacht, and children can't go because they get in the way of the ruddy boom. Today the men in the sailing trousers will have to move fast, changing tack around and around the choppy course, going about, going around and around seaweed-heavy buoys. I couldn't go with him today, I might fall in and drown, and nobody would realize until they got back to the moorings and they'd say, 'Damn it! I knew there was something . . .'

Today my father inhabits a separate world, a water world, full of ghosts whose hair rises up from the napes of their necks and touches the ceiling, and whose eyes stare open all the time.

Today, instead of spending the day with him, my mother and I will walk up to the top of the road to Maureen's Hair Emporium. I'm happy. I like Maureen's Hair Emporium.

My mother joins the throng of women who, in anticipation maybe of a sparkling Babycham or a vodka and lemonade later on that evening in the lounge bar right across the road from the shops, climb up the linoleum stairs above the grocery to Maureen's Hair Emporium for a shampoo and set.

There, resting their heads back into Maureen's tilted pink sink, they breathe in the heady scent of blue cigarette smoke and mauve peroxide paste. On this balmy autumn Saturday, they bask in the grown-up freedom of their new suburban lives. This is the beginning, this city suburb a new frontier. There is no room for inconvenient memory under Maureen's helmet-like hairdryers, no need to think back to shit-stained cows and flooded fields and cantankerous mothers and lascivious fathers and feral priests and worn-out shoes. This is the life. This is the future someone might have dreamed of in a cold girlhood bed, under a beady-eyed virgin, arms tight to her shivering sides.

Mainly I like Maureen's Hair Emporium because I like the mad smell of ammonia, and as well as that I mainly like seeing the neighbours beheaded by the tilting sink and disappearing under the hairdryers. But even more than those mainlys, I mainly like Maureen's bundle of magazines, which are for Customers' Use Only.

My mother's hair used to be black, and then she had babies. Now she prefers it to be the colour of bulrushes and straw. Maureen puts a rubber hat on my mother's head. The hat is perforated with tiny holes. Maureen pulls bits of my mother's hair through the holes, with a crochet needle, until my mother is decorated with a halo of stringy hair growing out of the rubber cap, and looks like she has been electrocuted.

Maureen paints the exposed hair with purple peroxide from her mixing bowl. Then we all read our magazines until the purple gets washed off. Then Maureen pulls off the rubber hat (a lot of wincing) and rolls up the newly yellowish hair in tiny little rollers, with elastic bands attached to keep them in place. Then she pours the setting lotion on top, and then my mother sits under one of Maureen's big hairdryer helmets, and then we read our magazines again. Then, when my mother is done, Maureen says 'You're cooked', which makes Maureen laugh every time. Maureen pushes up the helmet lid and sits my mother in front of the mirror. Sometimes Maureen goes to make a cup of tea then, or answer the telephone, and my mother sits still in front of Maureen's big mirror and looks at herself as if she's daring the herself in Maureen's mirror to say something.

When Maureen comes back, she back-combs and back-combs and back-combs with her fast little metal comb, and then she sprays my mother's hair with lacquer from the gold tin, until the hair is so hard that it is solid, immovable. Gales could blow, howling winds could howl, the earth could open and serpents could spit fire at us from their snaky mouths, and her hair would remain impervious.

Jesus was impervious – they rolled a boulder in front of his tomb, to trap him inside for eternity, and he just rolled it right back again and ascended into heaven anyway.

*

We walk back home down the dust-white road, so that my newly streaked mother can have an Aspirin.

'What's venereal disease?' I ask, following along behind the clack-clack-clack of my mother's slingbacks.

I am trying not to breathe too much, so as not to lose the fabulous, blasting scent of peroxide in my nostrils, but this is a burning question that demands immediate asking.

'What's venereal disease?' I ask again.

The blonder she is, the faster she walks.

'Venereal disease? What is it? Is it deadly? Can you die from it? If you got it, would you be dead? How long would you be alive before you were dead?'

Her ash-blonde head stiffens on top of her propelling shoulders. She stops outside our gate.

In next door's front garden, on the puddle of grass, the baby girls are pulling themselves up to standing, against the pram chassis. Their chubby fists reach up for the latest sister cradled inside.

Come out, little baby, come out and play.

I want to swallow the venereal-disease words down again, make them dissolve in ammonia.

'Who told you about venereal disease?' My mother's voice is low and still. She speaks in black and white, like the television.

'Angela Macnamara.'

'Who?'

'She is the aunt in agony in *Woman's Way*.'

'You were supposed to be reading *Twinkle*.'

'I finished it.'

We go inside, cross the tiny porch, shimmy down

the narrow hall past the sunburst mirror, nod to the fat telephone, push open the kitchen door. No one is home.

There are no Aspirin in the kitchen drawer. She pours a glass of water. Maybe they are next to her bed. I follow my mother upstairs into her bedroom. The two divans, the candlewick bedspreads, the rose-covered curtains, the dressing table and mirror the engine of the room. She finds the Aspirin in her make-up drawer, next to her eyelashes. She places the tablets right at the back of her throat, holding the pills at the tips of her red nails, opening her mouth as wide as it can open. I can see her teeth. Her all-the-better-to-eat-you-with teeth.

She swallows down the pills and inspects her roots, twirls the dry blonde hair between her fingertips. She is looking in the glass for such a long time it is impossible to know what she sees.

'I'd like to see what advice Angela Macnamara has to offer in this situation,' she says, as if I'm actually supposed to know what she is talking about. What situation, I want to ask, but the word situation is not friendly, and nobody will tell me anyway.

'I'd like to see Angela sink her gums into this,' she says to the mirror, which seems to be holding up its end of the conversation just fine.

I change tack. Changing tack is what you do on Dawn's dad's yacht when you want to go in another direction and everyone has to duck and the children have to get out of the ruddy way of the ruddy boom.

I will abandon venereal disease to the unaskable-questions bin. The unaskable-questions bin is getting quite full. The most recent question I put in it is why the alarm clock, which used to be plugged in between my mother's and father's beds, ended up lying in the middle of the back garden one morning last week, looking really really confused. Someone had thrown it out of my parents' bedroom window and it landed underneath the washing line. Thrown out, cast aside, abandoned, expelled, banished. It had done something unforgivable.

It is very very difficult now to know how late we are going to be for school, now that we don't have an alarm clock to ignore. Given the unfriendliness of the gabardine fishes, not to mention Sister Celestine's pinched and worried face, someone should have brought it back inside, or maybe not thrown it out in the first place.

Norah and I go out to visit the clock. It looks happy enough from the front, but Norah says it is suffering from 'catastrophic internal injuries'. Norah sometimes has to go to hospital, like if she gets a cold, sometimes for a whole week, so that she can breathe better when she comes out.

She knows quite a lot about injury.

'Me? Alarming?' croaks the blue clock, its gold hands fluttering over its startled face. 'Me? I thought they *wanted* to know the time. I thought they *wanted* me to herald the dawn. It doesn't feel quite *right*, lying out here under the sun and the stars.'

My mother is looking in the glass for such a long time it is impossible to know what she sees. I have thought of a change of tack. I will snap my mother out of her dream by telling her about a different article from *Woman's Way*, Ireland's Favourite Women's Magazine. I will tell her all about the article I had read on Maureen's leatherette couch while the wall-clock counted out the minutes and my mother's hair turned pale yellow.

This week, as 'A Welcome Bonus', *Woman's Way* has introduced 'Double Harness, A Brand New Series', in which famous Irish couples speak about their enthralling existences.

The article, I explain to my strangely defeated-looking mother, offers insights into the couples' lives. Like parables, or fingerprints, insights leave us important clues. 'Double Harness', I explain, for its first foray into exploring the heady lives of the rich and famous living on our shy island, spoke to 'The Gay Byrnes'.

'Mr and Mrs The Gay Byrnes go out for a stroll around town at two or three o'clock in the morning,' I tell my mother's blonde head. 'The Gay Byrnes say that is a lovely time to go for a walk. They have a roomy and spacious flat on the south side of the city, although they don't actually intend it to be their permanent home.'

The south side gets her attention. When my father's father was very ill, my mother and I hurried through the south side of the city on the way to the small hospital where he lay in a high bed, thirsty and cracked. The south side put a swing in my mother's step; it was the right place to be with a beauty spot and patent-leather high heels and sable-coloured nylons and a head full of ash-blonde streaks.

My mother looks at me from inside the wing-mirrored glass.

I see her image left, right and centre, six eyes, three mouths. Father, Son and Holy Ghost. She flickers with interest like a frightened moth. This is good tack-changing.

'And Mrs Gay Byrne did a corner-blue cookery course in London. And when they have dinner parties, she likes to serve coke-in-a-van. But during the week they just eat steak-and-kidney pudding.'

Gay Byrne is the biggest star in the country, bigger than President de Valera, who even has his own skipping song. Gay Byrne is the host of *The Late Late Show*, a Saturday-night television chat show, which is the cornerstone of the country's social and cultural life, at least that's what it said in the magazine. Everyone watches *The Late Late Show*, unless they are in The Club waiting for their husbands to finish the lined-up pints and drive them home.

Gay Byrne is a very likeable chap, said the magazine. Gay Byrne is married to a red-haired harpist called Kathleen. Kathleen used to be a continuity announcer on the television.

And who, in the name of God, doesn't want to be a continuity announcer?

'Kathleen knows how to sweat onions. That's what she learned on her corner-blue course. Also, they're going to France for their holidays. They're just going to drive around for a while, see where the fancy takes them. Maybe pop over to the Eiffel Tower and then maybe go for a swim.'

I am making the last bit up. In truth, the interview was a bit short on detail.

There is no clock in the bedroom, no tick-tock presence to measure out the time, only the slow, shallow emptiness of a Saturday afternoon, and a long, empty garden beyond the short rose-festooned curtains.

My mother, mother, mother, one, two, three, looks at me from inside the glass. 'Cordon bleu,' she says, quietly. 'Cordon bleu.'

My mother should have been a continuity announcer. She would have been happy if she'd been a continuity announcer. Because even air hostesses (who are definitely the next best thing to be), awash with bottles of 4711 and dashing co-pilots, want to be on the television. Even air hostesses, with drawers full of seamless stockings and wardrobes full of pencil skirts, air hostesses with flick-up eyeliner and pale-pink mouths and navy-blue court shoes and generous taxi allowances, they all want to be on the television. And if air hostesses who touch down in Rome, who see London three times a week, who know hotel lobbies like the backs of their manicured hands, if even those cherished, envied few want to be continuity announcers, then my mother certainly, absolutely, cross-your-heart-and-hope-to-die-ly, would have been happy if she had been a continuity announcer on the television.

And here's a secret to go into the very bottom of the unanswerable-questions bin, to hide under all those wonderings. Even nuns want to marry Gay Byrne. Even if it means being mouthless souls for the rest of eternity.

I go outside, lie on the dry grass. It's strange to be home on Saturday, to be beached in my own back garden. Everything feels quiet and still. I wonder what Dawn is doing, I wonder is she lying in her back garden looking at the sky, wondering when her father will come home in the big creamy car. Wondering where he is now.

The man next door is extremely tall. He is a policeman.

53

He is married to the smiling lady with all the spongy baby girls. His job is to protect President de Valera, I don't know from what. Today the man next door is pruning his roses. He is like a giant in fairyland. I think he is a very nice and kind man, but I bet he doesn't know how to sweat onions.

I think the problem, the really big problem, with Angela Macnamara's problem page is that she doesn't explain anything. Angela just gets flustered and outraged, and I imagine her shouting behind the typed-up answers to the readers' letters. Shouting and slamming her paper door loudly.

'Trial Marriages Lead to Venereal Disease!' roars Angela (without saying what it actually is).

'And there is to be no more about it!' says Angela.

'And what's more,' says Angela, 'if you haven't the decency to respect yourself, how is some poor boy, all excited in the back of a borrowed motor car, going to respect you? Answer me that!' says Angela. Crossly.

'We all know,' says Angela (and now she's speaking hard and low in the typed-up column), 'that men are not able to control their desires, and it's up to us to control them for them.'

The man next door nods at me over the fence, then clips his secateurs together and hurries inside in his gardening shoes to the wakeful strains of a hot-gummed toddler.

'No rest for the wicked,' he says, to no one in particular. 'No rest for the wicked.'

*

3

Pals

THERE IS A NEW NUN IN FRONT OF THE BLACKBOARD. She is called Sister Mary Immaculate. Immaculate means everything folded up and put away nicely, and the floor swept under your bed.

Sister Mary Immaculate wears glasses that swoop up at the sides like trapped birds trying to fly off her face. She is terribly worried about a great number of things, including multiplication and division, and the marks on our souls from misdemeanours we may have already accidentally committed, now that we are aged six, and some of us almost seven.

We need absolutely utterly immaculate souls for our First Holy Communion, which we will make on the tenth of May. God willing. You have to say 'God willing' after you make plans out loud, in case God gets a bit huffy and says: 'Oh yeah? Tenth of May, is it? And who are you? The cat's mother?'

I'm not sure who the cat's mother is supposed to be. I know, however, that I'm not the cat's mother. In order to be the cat's mother, you'd have to be a cat, even if you did get your baby from an angel.

The tenth of May is a Saturday, which might cause problems, as my Saturdays are taken. Booked. And, anyway, things have got pretty busy on Saturdays. My mother's Hospital Chorus is hitting the high notes. She's brought Judy Collins to the table and now, as well as wearing a plaited wig and drawing freckles all over her nose and putting on wire-rimmed spectacles over her false eyelashes, and singing 'Three Little Maids from School' to the sick and the mad, she and three other members of the chorus have formed a band called Four in a Bar. Mainly to sing the ice-cream song, the castles-in-the-air song.

'Four in a Bar?' says my father. 'Not a particularly popular spot then?'

The eggs are spending more time airborne than on the ruddy plate these days. I'm not sure what ruddy means, but it's nice to say. Ruddy ruddy ruddy ruddy.

On Saturdays my mother packs up her 'Three Little Maids from School' costume, and her eyeliner, and her platform shoes, and her eyelashes, and her bellbottoms and her bolero, and waits at the window with her black suitcase for her friend Ed. Ed plays guitar in Four in a Bar and he is a very good driver. When Ed pulls up, with his neat beard and his sheepskin car coat, and the other two little maids from school in the back seat, one of whom is his wife, and a worried-looking tenor called Tom, riding shotgun, my mother waves gaily to them all out the window, and then rushes down the path and into Ed's square car.

Sometimes, if my father is racing on Dawn's father's

yacht, and there's no one to mind me, I go with her. But the wooden seats lined up in the hospital recreation rooms, and the sad old people sitting in them, rocking back and forwards and forwards and back long before the concert has even started, make me feel frightened. And one evening there is a young girl in the front row, holding a doll and waiting quietly . . . at least I think she is a little girl because of her ankle socks and party dress, but her face is old and dry, and when I stare at her, which you're not supposed to do, she spits at me.

I sit as far away from her as I can, also in the front row, on the very edge, but even though I am not looking at her, I can still see her.

I know all the words my mother sings. I know the words to the Judy Collins song where she's turning and turning and turning, and the one where she's standing still looking at the clouds. My father always says that there's nothing quite as depressing as an Irish tenor, so he probably wouldn't like anxious Tom's rendition of 'Will Ye Go, Lassie, Go?', a song which goes on for such a long time that the lassie would probably be well back by now, and have her feet up in front of *Quicksilver*.

Anyway, if my father thinks Irish tenors are depressing, it's because he's never actually seen an old lady rocking a doll.

Afterwards, when my mother and her friends are finished singing and doing their party pieces, and the audience have been put back into bed, even though it's still bright outside, the nuns give the sopranos and light tenors, and the tambourine rattlers, and the reliable guitarists, cups of tea and ham sandwiches without crusts, and iced fairy cakes and lemon drizzle cake, and tell the performers that they are all little rays of sunshine, God's sunshine.

SOME SATURDAYS, CERTAIN UNPREDICTABLE SATURDAYS, are different. They are unique Saturdays. Extraordinary Saturdays. Which means that they are not likely to happen again for absolutely ages and ages and ages.

On those breath-catch Saturdays, the car rolls out of our bleached housing estate and turns right, away from the sea and the gulls and The Club, and out on to the big wide flat road to the city. And the coins jingle in my father's pocket and the hot, oily car hums with happiness, and soon it is whinnying and snorting and shaking its locks and kicking up the dust and driving us fast, and there is just me and him, and we are free. Free as gulls.

In the city, we park on unfamiliar streets, disembark, criss-cross wide pavements, past long, tall houses with balconies and railings and big stone steps. We move like silky wool in and around and up and over the big grey town, cruising on into the cavernous gallery on the square.

Inside, we glide from silent room to silent room, on skiddable wooden floors, looking at the pictures hanging on the forest-green walls. We look and look and look at the people in the frames: the dead men with ugly moustaches; the dead women with no eyebrows; the dead birds plucked clean on wooden tables; the dead children staring straight at us, trapped in lace and velvet; the dead dogs at their feet. And then we go downstairs and order cake in the dark cafe underneath the ground.

He watches while I eat. Often he listens to me, but he also often gets distracted by the sword that is hanging over his head.

I've never actually seen the sword, which apparently used to hang over someone called Damocles, but I can see it in my mind. I suspect my father would be an awful lot happier if Damocles came back from wherever he went (possibly a very long holiday in Greece) and took his place, so that my father could stop thinking the sword was going to fall on top of him and slice his ruddy head off.

There is a strawberry on my chocolate cake. I will save it till last. Like God does when Jesus miracles up a damn good bottle.

That's what he did at the wedding feast at Cana. There are drawings of it in our religion book, and there are paintings in the gallery of the dead. The pictures show the Apostles wearing striped robes and sandals, with long, leather thongs wrapped around their legs, exactly the sort the drowned lady wore.

Jesus is also there, wearing a white robe, stroking his beard, checking the sun-dial and looking around to make sure everything is going all right. Jesus is not really a party person.

During the wedding feast, the host runs out of wine, and there is none lined up. The guests are thinking about moving on somewhere else, maybe to a hotel, because hotel bars don't close at lunchtime. But Jesus quietly slips outside and turns jugs and jugs and jugs of water into wine, and everyone is delighted.

'You have saved the best wine until last,' the guests

cheer, and the host winks at Jesus, and the night is a big success.

Jesus played a blinder.

'They are all dead,' I say. 'All the people in all the paintings, the people with the togas and the veils and the robes and the riding boots and the sandals that criss-cross up their legs. And all the spaniels, and all the little girls with ringlets and gloves, and all the flowers by their feet, and even the cats who live nine times. Everyone in this whole gallery is dead.'

'You're alive,' he says. 'Eat your strawberry.'

We need to quit this crazy scene. Go outside, pull up the collar of our corduroy jacket, shake an untipped cigarette from the box, put it between our thin, dry lips, exhale, look up at the scudding grey-pink clouds, low and dense over Dublin city.

We need to hurry down Grafton Street, slip in and out between the shuddering, belching, open-mouthed buses, past window displays of plaster women in Easter dresses and big billowy hats. The models have plaster hands screwed on to their plaster arms, and sometimes the hands fall off, showing the big metal rods in their wrists. I've seen the same metal rods inside the statues of Mary and Joseph in my school, especially after Joan Brophy accidentally hit the May altar with her basketball. I wonder if the Virgin Mary would like a change of scenery? I wonder if she'd like to stand behind the glass in a floppy straw hat. I wonder if she'd like to pose, hand on plaster hip, with these great big dolls, looking out over the city? I wonder if she'd like to swap her sky-blue robes, just for a day or two, for a knee-length cocktail dress and a bolero?

The plaster women look way, way past us, into the distance. Maybe they can see something that we can't, with their flat, painted-on eyes.

We are not made of plaster, he and I, we are alive, we are on the Earth, we are made of flesh and bone and blood and guts; we are human, we don't have screws inside us.

We take a sharp turn down a sideways street, to a dark hotel. We need to hurry, we need to get to the heavy glass door, push it open, duck inside. It's raining harder now, big, sharp, straight-down, warm rain. We need to move fast but look slow. We need shelter from the mad hot rain and the dangerous sword, slipping out from under the black and pink clouds, the tip reaching down for us, stretching down down down through the fat raindrops, falling heavy and loud and dark now on this narrow glittery street.

The door opens, we elude the sword, hold on to our heads, just. We are escapologists, we are Houdinis; we cannot be bound, or chopped, or sliced clean in half. We have won, for now.

We sink into the lobby, where our footsteps are absorbed by the mustard-coloured carpet and where my outdoor shoes look embarrassed by their scuff.

'Maybe we shouldn't be here,' whisper my shoes. 'This is a different sort of world entirely.'

'It's fine,' he says, when I squeeze his hand into a question mark. 'It's fine.' He smiles with the front of his face. We have blue eyes, the same eyes.

'Who's Billy's pal?'

'Daddy is,' I whisper.

'Who's Daddy's pal?'

'Billy is.'

We straighten up our shoulders, wipe the sweat from our top lips, clear our smoky throats, walk into the bar.

In the hotel the talk is low, the talk rumbles. The men doing the talking are smooth as glass. The pink veins on their noses are hidden under suntans. They have fat brown cigarettes in silver cases, and heavy ink pens to sign their cheques. Their drinks come iced on silver trays. They probably won't be jumping up and down and saying, 'Your round, you bastard.'

The men we are meeting are gathered by the bar, wearing suits and laughing from deep behind their shirt buttons.

They are curious to meet my father. They make a space for him, nod at the barman who isn't Frank, and a pint is pulled. I watch it settle on the countertop, watch the sand rise up from the tall black sea. I hold on to the back of my father's leg, refuse a stool or a fizzy orange. I will be as still as the little dead girls in the frames, unblinking, silent. I will imagine a dead dog at my feet.

There were no cameras in the olden days. If the little girls wanted to be remembered in their party clothes, they had to stand still for days and weeks and months and years.

One of the smooth men kneels down to speak to me.

'Who have we got here?' he says, sounding but not looking friendly. He smiles big and wide; his gums are white. Maybe he has scurvy; you can get scurvy from not eating your greens.

We have important business here. There is a promise

in the air. If the promise is kept, Damocles will have to sit up and think about reclaiming his place under his ruddy sword.

The suntanned men in the mirror-shiny shoes want my father to draw picture postcards that will be sold in America. And if that happens, we will have wherewithal. Just like all the other people my father likes to spend his time with.

If we had money, had wherewithal, my father would stop trying to figure things out all the time. He has to do so much figuring out he doesn't get home until nearly eleven o'clock in the night-time. He'd stop looking for his chequebook everywhere, and fingering the coins in his pocket, and pocketing the bills from the taxman, and massaging the back of his neck in irritation when the neighbours pop up from behind the hedge, with a pair of gardening shears in their hands, saying,

'Thanks be to God for the day that's in it.'

Those aren't good words to say to my father. If he had wherewithal he would live right on the edge of the beach and have two Labradors, and a faded carpet under a long window, and a brass poker and a hostess trolley, and he'd be a Protestant.

My father would prefer if he'd been a Protestant in the first place, like his own father. But his mother wouldn't let him; she is from Kerry, and she has narrow lips and hair that looks like you could blow it away and tell the time by how many puffs it takes to make her bald. She has red lips and yellow teeth and her room in the home is narrow and smells like medicine. She stays in bed all day with a hot-water bottle and a naggin of whiskey and ten untipped Player's cigarettes, and when we go to see her she looks surprised and says, 'Go away and I'll give you ten bob.'

The main thing about my father's mother, besides her narrow mouth, and the air between her and her son in her narrow nursing-home room, which feels like no air, which feels like soup air, which feels like you really need air, is that when he was a little boy she told my father to wear short pants and be a Catholic.

My father's father, my Protestant grandfather, is dead. He was pale yellow when he died in the big iron hospital bed. Protestants don't believe in Mary, no matter which name she is using. Protestants don't go to heaven when they die, and float around as mouthless souls. They go somewhere else, maybe to a meeting.

'Protestants are people who make very good jam,' my father says when I ask him what exactly Protestants are.

'And chutney,' he adds, facing into the long bedroom mirror, folding his green silk handkerchief into a narrow triangle, standing it upright in the breast pocket of his donkey-brown corduroy jacket.

As well as making very good jam, Protestants also have nicer teeth and, as well as that, they have canteens of cutlery and electric blankets, and some of them have colour televisions and ponies. And they are gentle and kind, and they have factory-knitted cardigans with arms that are the same length and buttons opposite the actual buttonholes, not like cardigans some mothers knit at home, which can be a bit lopsided and unreliable. Protestant ladies even have twin-sets, which means a jumper and a cardigan that match. Twin-sets come in nice pale colours, in blues and pinks and lemony yellows, the same colours as our teacups.

Those are just some of the reasons why I think my father wants to be a Protestant, but it's also to do with the alphabet. Protestants say 'aitch' for H, and Catholics say 'haitch' for H. There aren't that many rules in our house, but one rule is to always say aitch and also to say the word film like 'filmmm', not 'fillum'. The other rules are to chew with your mouth closed and to cut your toast into triangles.

My father would like to be a Protestant with two surnames and a soft-top car and a house with a sea view, where the only person with a pair of sun-glint shears, hopping out from behind the hedge to say 'Soft day, thanks be to God', would be the gardener.

'Dream on,' says my mother, biting the thread between her teeth to sew the loose button on to his sports jacket. 'Ream on.' She bought patches in Hickey's fabric shop to sew on to his sleeves.

Most of the people my father sails with have lots of money. So much money, so much wherewithal, that they spend it on bigger sailing boats and more brown-eyed ponies and lots and lots of outdoor shoes. And they go on actual airplanes. They fly to small islands where people give them their lunch on the beach, and where it's hot enough to wear a toga, if you had a toga, if anyone has a toga any more.

There is a girl called Zoe (which is probably the best name in the entire universe) who sometimes comes into The Club with her brown-skinned father, although not often, not often enough to sit on the window seat with me and Dawn and join in our important conversations. Zoe lives in a white house with black timber decorating the outside, and a red roof on top, like from a fairy tale, and she has a television in her bedroom and a terrapin. Apparently.

And both of those facts are pretty extraordinary.

'One day,' he says. 'Some day.'

'Ream on,' says my mother, biting the thread between her white white teeth. 'Ream on and on and on.'

The men in the suits, who have sharp lines down the middle of their trouser legs, are talking to my father in the hotel bar because he is the best at drawing. He is an artist. That is his job. He used to work in an advertising agency, drawing other people's ideas for them. But then someone said that he should have his own business, drawing people's big ideas on his own, and maybe colouring them in as well. And the same someone said that my father would surely make lots of money, and when he did, he could drive cars that started as soon as you turned the key in the ignition. Also, he could put things on tabs, which is a fun thing to do, and he could eat his dinner in dark hotels with white linen tablecloths, and he could even hold a little hammer in his fist to crack open shells. Because people with lots of money and lots of wherewithal like to eat things that come in shells.

'You're a creative!' said the someone with the big ideas. 'How fucking creative can you be on the money you're on? Tell me that? Eh? Eh?'

My father left the advertising agency, and drove home

early in a silver car that smelt of polish and heat, which the person with the big ideas said he was allowed to have now that he was a company director of his very own company.

'Walnut dash,' he said, while I sat on his knee in the driver's seat and pushed the pedals up and down. Across the road, Celine O'Flaherty was swinging on her garden gate, looking at us like she wanted to cast bad spells. I didn't care; she never let me play in her wigwam anyway.

Everyone was almost happy for about three days, but later the car disappeared, and so did the person with the splendid ideas. And then more bills spilled from the postman's fingers and landed in the hallway, and squadrons of cooked sausages flew around the kitchen like they had wings.

'He was damn short on detail, your entrepreneurial friend,' hissed my mother, lying on her bed with two slices of cucumber over her eyelids. 'Damn short.'

'Paddy McGinty's goat!' says a rumble-voiced, shiny-shoed man at the hotel bar.

It's the man with the wide white gums. I've been watching him sucking on a segment of lime. 'Can you draw Paddy McGinty's goat?' scurvy man says to my father, while I watch the sharp line of his suit break at the knee.

'Yes, yes, of course.'

Of course my father can draw goats. He can draw goats and donkeys, and horses that look like ballerinas, and cows with long eyelashes and delicate little ankles. He can draw the faces of all the people on the top deck of the bus, and all the people hurrying down the street under their umbrellas. He can draw little girls in school uniforms, and gnarled old priests, and rickety nuns in wimples. He can make pictures where there used to be nothing but blankness, where there used to just be empty white paper with nothing to see or hold on to.

'You can, can you? Can you draw a goat?'

'Yes, of course. I can draw McGinty's goat, any goat you like,' answers my father. And that seems to settle it, because another round is ordered and I watch his pint blacken and rise again, and then I see him look over his shoulder to see what will happen next. And after a little while the rumble-shine men run out of words, they stop saying 'New York' and 'Chicago' and 'Paddy McGinty' and 'fair fucks', and begin to row away, across the carpet, and that's when the yellow-haired lady, the 'so-that's-who-you-are' lady, drifts over to the bar.

She is nearly always somewhere.

The last of the men pack away the end of their words, they shake my father's hand and walk their legs out of the door, and what happens next is that it's just her and him and me. She smiles at me.

'Hello,' she says, and she calls me by my written-down name, which is handy, because that's a name I don't really have to own.

Her face is so difficult to hold in my mind. Even when I look at her, it is as if she is hiding behind water. Her features are indistinct, pale, blonde. She is there and she is not there; she is waiting behind herself. She touches the back of his sports jacket, folds down his collar that he had turned up against the sudden rain, before we ran through the sword-heavy streets. Her hands are blue-white, her veins turquoise. She is long and slow and pale and yellow; she is like a very important word you can't quite remember, or the possibility of sun behind a cloud. She is fleeting, you think you've got her, and then she is gone. She is a snowdrift.

She touches the place where his jacket button used to be loose. Her eyes ask him a question.

And now we are to leave the hotel, and I still haven't moved or spoken.

We drive again, but not home. We follow behind snow-drift's low car, out out out of the city. Past the turn-off to our estate, and all the way to the seafront hotel. All the way back out to the corner of our world, to where the sea interrupts the earth. To the white hotel that doesn't close at lunchtime or at night-time, where the salt water stains the glass.

'Who's Daddy's pal?' he asks me when we've parked, breaking the silence.

'Billy is,' I answer quietly.

Because there is only one answer.

The snowdrift lady will meet us there, in the bar, and she might even bring her little golden dog on his red lead, and I can walk him around the hotel garden. I can walk him around and around the long garden, on my own, with the stretched black trees, and the washed-up seaweed, and the twigs and pine cones, and the splintered driftwood, all crushed up and scattered over the grass.

All scratchy and broken and uneven, all torn up and misplaced and thrown around by the storm.

The pale yellow lady's dog is called Sandy. Her name is Eve.

Eve. Eve was the first woman in the world, the one made out of a rib, the one who woke up the snake because she couldn't resist the apple, the one who called up all the locusts and spat out the tempests.

Later, driving home in the car, under the wet pools of street light, he lets me change gear.

'Third,' he instructs, putting his foot on the pedal. 'Fourth. Third again.'

He is happy. Maybe the goat men cheered him up.

'We should go on a holiday,' he says.

'Will we wear togas?' I ask.

'Maybe.'

We turn into our road.

'Second,' he says. 'First.'

We park the car in the puddle of tarmac, in front of our garage door. We turn off the engine. The stars are already out.

'Who did we not see today?' he asks.

I look at him, but I know the answer to that question is not to answer that question. Not out loud. It isn't really a question anyway, it's a code, and we understand codes. We are one. We are pals.

4

Bye Bye, Nigel

I F YOU LOOK UP FROM OUR GARDEN GATE, YOU SEE TWO windows, one into the big bedroom, which is Louise and Anna's room, and the other into the box bedroom, which is John's room. If you look carefully at the big bedroom window, you can see a little hole, low down, in the corner of the glass. The little hole was made one night by one of the sharp pebbles that Anna throws at the window to wake Louise up. Then Louise creeps down the stairs, and opens the front door, so that Anna can sneak inside and go to bed and think about Georgie Wilson and the wet sand on her back.

Louise and Anna can't really see me, they only talk to each other. As well as talking to each other, they also iron each other's hair under sheets of brown paper, so that it's straight instead of curly. Also, they have arguments about who owns which pair of tights. Once they screamed and screamed and screamed, because Louise borrowed Anna's black woollen trousers and cut the ends off them with the kitchen scissors, so that they would fit into her knee-high boots. But the trousers unravelled and unravelled until there were no trousers left, and Anna cried because she had spent a whole week's wages on them, because they were groovy.

Louise and Anna wear night-and-day dresses, which are quite long dresses called midis. Night-and-day dresses can be worn in bed and then straight up to the shops in the morning, which is handy if you are in a hurry. Anna wears her dress to go up to the newsagent's at the top of the road, to buy ten Major cigarettes in the military-green packets. Louise wears her dress to stride around the block and get some air, and to sit on the garden wall and wait for her boyfriend, who is a Protestant, to pick her up in his Mini. His Mini is a car, not a dress, though there are also mini dresses in Louise and Anna's wardrobe. Sometimes they wear their minis instead of their midis, or their hot pants with their fishnet tights underneath, when they go to dances. To 'hops', which are dances, and not always on one leg. Louise and Anna's clothing life is very complicated. Louise and Anna are very complicated.

'Exotic,' says Norah when we creep into their bedroom, which always has the curtains closed. We open up their wardrobe door, unleashing their belts and scarves, and boots with fringes, and their two kaftans that came from Morocco, and their one furry, embroidered coat that might have been a llama once and smells like a wet dog.

My siblings speak in whispers because they have very important things to say to each other. They are all fruit of my mother's womb, that's a certainty, although who else was involved is a mystery. Surely their father cannot be the same person as my father? There's only room for two on our team. Him and me. Daddy and Billy. Pals.

The hole that the sharp pebble made in my sisters' window splintered the glass, like a bullet hole, like an entry wound. After a few weeks, when the window still hasn't been fixed, Louise takes out her red nail polish and follows the splintered lines with the little brush. She paints them in, in pillar-box red. Now the cracked glass looks like a war zone.

'I suppose it's artistic,' says our smiling neighbour with the multiplying baby girls.

Louise is sixteen now and Anna is fifteen. They wait together at the bus stop on the main road to get the open-backed bus into town, so that they can go to work. Anna quickly smokes the end of her cigarette as the bus comes into sight, drawing the smoke down down down inside her, making it last until her break time. Until she can have another one, out the back of the hair salon, where she works as a junior.

Louise doesn't smoke. Louise just looks up at the tree-tops and the scuddy sky, and thinks about air and space and silence and what it would be like to draw the clouds and colour in the air. Mainly Louise likes to open windows and breathe and think. Louise doesn't like to sit upstairs where the smokers sit, which is why Anna has to smoke fast at the bus stop.

Anna started working in a hairdressing salon beside the seaside when she was fourteen, sweeping up the ladies' dead hair and pouring peroxide into mixing bowls and finding people's coats under the stairs, before they dashed out into the rain with their hoods up over their shampoo and set. Her job was to sweep the floor all day and wash peroxide down the sink. She also had to pull at the ladies' wobbly heads with a crochet needle. Anna changed jobs, and now she works in a hairdressing shop in the city and makes enough money to buy cigarettes and bracelets and Sloopy jeans and unravelling trousers and turquoise hot pants. On Friday nights she also uses some of her tip money to buy me a big bar of brazil-nut chocolate. This is pretty fantastic. Anna used to go to school, but that was before the expulsion.

So far, Louise has had two different jobs that she didn't like. One was in a fur shop in the city centre, but she hated all the little dead minks looking at her with dead eyes, and there were no windows to open in the musty shop, and there was no fresh air, just powdery old ladies coming through the door and stroking the coats. So my father found her a job, of sorts, in an advertising agency. But they don't really know what to do with her there. Sometimes she cuts out different-shaped letters from a sheet of Letraset for the ad men to stick down on their clean white pages. Sometimes she makes the copywriters cups of milky coffee, and sometimes she goes outside and sits on the big granite steps, trying to get some air. Sometimes, when the copywriters and the graphic artists and the creatives (who are guys that sit around chewing the ends of their felt-tip pens and fingering their moustaches) run out of things for her to do, they stand her up in the paper bin, full of cut-up paper shapes and unwanted notions.

Maybe they do this because she has long auburn hair, and green eyes, and she looks more interesting in the bin than their rejected concepts.

Louise and Anna go to work every single day except Sunday, even on Saturdays.

The nuns said they couldn't go to school any more because they knew too much about boys and they went to hops. The nuns expelled Louise and Anna from the convent. Expelled means pushed out, never to return. When they came home for the last time in their grey uniforms, with their hardly used books in their bags and the word 'expelled' sitting on their thin shoulders, nobody really did anything about it. My parents, their parents (if they are the same two people), mainly seem to have forgotten to send them to another school.

Louise and Anna sat on the stairs looking a little bit scared, and then they got jobs, and my mother lay in the bath humming the cloud song. Maybe all those clouds and moons and dunes and Ferris wheels got in the way of deciding what to do with her daughters.

Expulsion is the very worst thing that can happen. It's a right kick in the teeth for the Virgin Mary, make no mistake. Saint Patrick, who is the holy saint of our isle, and whose birthday we celebrate on St Patrick's Day, also expelled things. He expelled snakes from Ireland. You could search the length and breadth of this country, lift every rock, shine a light into every nook and cranny, and you'd still never find a snake. There are no snakes in Ireland. Not a single one. No vipers wriggling around like there's no tomorrow. We are Irish and we are snake-free. We are Saint Patrick's poor children, on whom he bestows a sweet smile, and expulsion is the worst thing that can happen to anyone. Expulsion means getting rid of something because it's useless and dangerous, and because it's evil.

'I don't know,' says Norah, when I tell her about Louise and Anna's expulsions. We are sitting in the porch outside my front door, waiting for Louise's Protestant boyfriend to pull up in his Mini, so we can check him to see if there are any giveaway black marks creeping up his neck from his soul. While we wait, we are also watching three wasps drown in the jam jar that Norah and I have filled with a lot of water and a little bit of jam.

'I don't know,' says Norah. 'I don't know if expulsion is the *worst* thing that can happen. I mean, you could be chased through a black wood by a one-eyed convict who is wrapped in filthy bandages, and then you could run into quicksand and sink without trace, and your lungs could fill up with sand. You could just die. That would definitely be worse than expulsion.'

She has a point.

MY BROTHER'S EYES ARE BROWN AND GREEN AT THE SAME time. He has dark-brown hair. He says that he is from my father as well as from my mother. I asked. We had a meeting, under the dining-room table, just like Protestants.

'Are you my actual brother?'

'Yes, and Anna and Louise are your actual sisters.'

'Both of them? Are you sure we are all from both of them?'

'Did you think there was a fucking alternative?'

Yes, I do think there is an alternative. I think my father and I are special. Untouchable. The only two members of a very select tribe. Maybe John has got it wrong. He is rolling up tiny cigarettes in see-through paper, under the canopy of the table.

John is still in school, although his days are numbered. 'Your days are numbered,' the priests have told him. When I ask him which number he is on now, and how many numbers are left, he doesn't know.

'I'm fucked,' he says.

It's not that I mind having siblings. I actually really like John, and our meetings under the table, and sitting very still beside his long-playing records listening to the Beatles.

'I like Paul McCartney,' I tell him.

'No you don't,' he says. 'You like John Lennon. If anyone asks you, you like John Lennon.'

'I don't like John Lennon. He has glasses. I like Paul McCartney.'

'I'm so fucked,' my brother says, licking the gluey strip of flimsy cigarette paper like my mother licks a stamp.

Joseph adopted Jesus, and when Jesus was growing up he gave him a job in his carpentry shop. The job was just sweeping up sawdust and varnishing jewellery boxes and bread bins; the small stuff. This was so that Jesus could pass for a normal human being and not attract the attention of Pontius Pilate (who wasn't a pilot at all, apparently, but who was a cruel leader).

I suppose I think that my father adopted my siblings, just like Joseph adopted Jesus. I suppose I think that I am different, that, for him, I wasn't a mistake, I was a good surprise.

*

Until recently, my brother has been going to a school run by people called Brothers, who aren't actually each other's brothers. They are boy nuns, and they live in the other big red-brick school that holds down our parish like a paperweight. Now the Brothers don't want John to go to school any more either.

In my brother's school, the Brothers often chat about giving the students a belt in the kisser. A belt in the kisser doesn't mean what it sounds like. A belt in the kisser is when someone smacks you hard in your mouth, because they don't like the words you're using or the ideas that are in your head. That has never happened to me, and it's not allowed to happen in my school. In my school, the nuns aren't allowed to hit us. That's why my father pays fees for me to go to school, when he can find his chequebook. He pays fees for the not-hitting bit, and for our soup-and-a-roll at lunchtime.

There is a national school across the road from our convent. Most of my friends who live on my estate go to the national school, where the uniform is green and red tartan. The nuns in my school say that we are not allowed to walk home with the national school girls, that we are not allowed to mix with those girls when we are in uniform, that those girls aren't special, their fathers don't pay fees, that our grey uniform makes us special, important. Sometimes I walk home with my friends who live on my road, but we obey the rules and we don't talk until I have gone home, run up the stairs and changed into my own clothes, before dashing back out to the road with a banana sandwich to play hopscotch and sit on the wall and talk about wedding dresses and dogs.

The Brothers in my brother's school are sometimes as good as their word, which is not very good at all. His school doesn't give a tuppenny bit whether you pay fees or not; he's going to get a belt in the kisser one way or the other.

My brother wrote a poem about a prostitute on the back of his Irish exam paper, and drew her too. Quite beautifully, with his ink pen, and the Brother finally snapped.

'I've finally snapped,' said the broken-clean-in-half Brother, reaching for his two stray legs.

Prostitutes are women who wear high heels and fishnet stockings and party shoes all day long, even if it's cold and raining, and my brother probably wrote a very good poem about them because he writes really good stories that he reads to me under the table, and poems are stories, only shorter. Anyway, the Brothers are seething, their leather straps are galloping out from under their cassocks and chasing my brother up and down the corridors. And they are just dying to give him buckets of belts in the kisser.

My brother hates his school; he hates the Brothers so much it makes his words shake and roll and crash out of his mouth all at the same time, like waves tearing over the ocean floor.

My father calls my brother into the kitchen to have a conversation about the prostitute poem. It doesn't go awfully well. The kitchen-table conversation begins with warts, which, like clouds that pour and rain, is probably not a good sign.

'You are a wart on my palm. Remove it.'

This is the first sentence: it is said by my father to my

brother. My father is the palm, my brother is the wart. I am just the other person at the table, sandals swinging above the tiled kitchen floor.

The yellow Formica-topped kitchen table is doing its best to navigate us through breakfast. Its four splayed legs are hanging on to the sea-green floor tiles. Head down to the wind, it rides the great waves that billow through the Polyester curtains and bounce off the Styrofoam ceiling. The table has passengers to protect, crew to consider; already the milk jug is quaking, the sugar bowl is trembling, the salt and pepper shakers are packing up their flavourings in invisible suitcases, preparing to flee.

'Come on, come on,' shouts Mr Pepper over the mad high whistle of the wind. 'Hurry up, hurry up, woman! The storm is here!'

My Rice Krispies list in the bowl like drowned things. Mayflies, one snap-crackle-and-pop and they are extinguished. I push them away, right into the eye of the storm.

'You. Are. A. Wart. On. My. Palm.'

My brother sits opposite my father, across the raging torrent of the yellow table. He is unrepentant. Unrepentant is an important word.

'Fuck them,' says my brother. 'Fuck them.'

The rashers are worriers; they huddle together on my father's plate. The sausages, who can be awful bullies, snigger up their sleeves. The mushrooms, always first with the news, wake up the grilled tomato, who is a bit slow on the uptake, a bit slovenly, and the egg, sunbathing in a shaft of dusty light from the stormy morning window.

'I just cannot be bothered with this nonsense one minute longer,' says the egg.

My mother is singing in the bath. Her voice drifts down the stairs and squeezes under the doorframe. She is singing loud, singing about ice-cream castles and Ferris wheels and dizzy dancing.

'Fuck them.' John pushes back on the kitchen chair.

If my sisters have a lot in common with the Poor Banished Children of Eve, my brother has a lot in common with unrepentant Eve herself, who looked well pleased with her forbidden apple. Eve was the first woman in the world. God made the world in seven days, and on the last day, at the end of a busy week, he remembered to make Eve.

'Damn it,' said God, when he had just sat down, 'I knew I'd forgotten something.'

And he flew back down to Earth and made Eve from some leftover rib that he hadn't needed for Adam. God waved his magic wand at it, and she grew around it. She grew into a human.

Adam was doing very well. He was up on his own two feet, hunting and foraging for wild berries and pineapples, making friends with chimps and fashioning hammocks out of vines and feasting on coconuts in the lovely, plentiful Garden of Eden. Adam didn't have a bad word to say about anybody, but then again there wasn't anybody to say a bad word about.

'Get out,' says my father to my brother. He says it quietly, quietly, quietly.

My brother's chair returns to earth. He stands, he picks up his cigarettes from the kitchen table.

The salt and pepper pots put down their bags, look at him and then at each other in nervous anticipation.

'What's happening now?' whispers Mrs Salt.

83

'Shush, woman,' says Mr Pepper. 'Stop your caterwauling.'

My brother places his hands on the table. His brown eyes are shiny and wide.

'It was fucking poetry.'

'Out,' says my father, closing his blue eyes in disdain. 'Out,' he whispers.

We roar like mice. We roar delicately. We are civilized people after all. When the kitchen door closes and the gale subsides, and Mrs Salt settles her skirts and mops her brow, my father picks up his cutlery and carefully removes the crispy edges from his terribly relieved rashers.

He passes the rind to me. I eat.

When my brother was a little boy he went to my school, until after his first Holy Communion. Then, because he was a big boy now, he went to the Brothers, and every day he was beaten with a leather strap, or a ruler, or a hard flat hand. He couldn't write his words straight down, the letters skated over the page and invented their own spellings. The Brothers didn't think that was interesting or important, they just thought it was bad and slothful and sinful and lazy and disrespectful and downright impudent. After the first year of trying and failing to make the letters stand together in word fortresses, and not spill over the page like crazy indians, after that first year of waiting for the crack of strap on his small palm, his words started to come out in rushes, falling over one another on to his desk.

'What is your name, boy?' the priest would ask, strap twitching.

'J-J-J-J-J-John,' he would say.

'And tell me, J-J-J-J-J-John,' the priest would say, carefully pushing down his cuticles with the sharp edge of his metal ruler, 'what magnificent contribution do you plan on making to this world? Eh? J-J-J-J-J-J-John.'

And that was how the priest showed John the John inside him. The J-J-J-J-J-John inside him. They stood him at the top of the class until they were ready to beat his small hands and his small legs, and prod his small shoulders with the butts of their nicotine-drenched fingers, and smack their holy hands around the crown of his delicate head and his small frozen face. They kept looking for John, even after they had hardened his green-brown eyes to small stones, and made the whistle of their straps the only music they could hear. They kept looking and looking, but they never found him.

'Fuck you,' says my brother, and that is the last thing said in the chat. And then my brother walks straight out the door, and I eat the rasher rind, and my mother sings in the bath. And in the hair salon, in the city, Anna sweeps up the dead hair from under the swivelling plastic seats and Louise stands in the wastepaper basket while the creative people decide what to do with her.

After the chat, I can't find John. Not anywhere, not in his room, or in the coal shed, or even mending his bicycle tyre in the garage with a basin of water and little rubber bandages, which is a thing he often does. I wait in our usual place under the dining-room table, but he never comes back.

Now nobody goes to school from our house any more. Just me.

IT'S SATURDAY EVENING. MY PARENTS ARE PREPARING to go out to The Club. My mother back-combs her hair with a steel comb and sprays hairspray hard into its centre. Then, like God after a heavy week of creation, she puts the Finishing Touch to her face: her eyebrows first, then the beauty spot, drawn on with her eyebrow pencil, above her chin and below her mouth. This is a delicate operation. First she pushes out the skin from the inside, with her little pink tongue, to make a hard surface, then she narrows her eyes in the glass, focuses on the point and twirls the eyebrow pencil around and around in tiny blunt circles.

'Inising utch.' Finishing touch.

I want to ask her where my siblings came from.

'Did you have a visit? Did an archangel knock on your window to tell you they were in your womb, although you didn't know it yet?' I only ask the questions inside my mind, behind my teeth, like a bad ventriloquist. 'Ere id ey fum rum?'

'Are you trying to sing?' she asks.

'No.'

'Are you choking?'

'No.'

I can't ask the questions out loud, they could boomerang back when I'm not looking and whip my ruddy head off.

Anyway, I don't sing. Ever.

*

When my mother was tasked with being the mother of my siblings, she tried very hard to keep on being a singer and an actress in musical comedy, which was her job. She tried to hold on to the way things used to be when she was having costumes delivered to her in wicker baskets, and flowers pinned to her delicate waist. But the stench of the nappies, and the babies' crawling, clawing limbs, knocked the music clean out of her. And soon she realized that she wasn't able to meet all those fabulous expectations that she had heard about herself in those exciting basket-opening days.

Then, when my siblings were old enough to walk and talk and find their own socks under their unmade beds and sprinkle their own sugar on their Progress Oatlets, she decided it was time to try again. Time to go out and look for all those disappeared promises, pick up on the trail of dusty expectations, follow each memory to see where it led, like Hansel and Gretel in the forest. This may not have been a great idea, however; maybe she forgot that Hansel and Gretel nearly ended up roasted alive in a witch's oven.

When my mother was ready to find her old self again, she ringed her mouth with carmine and went to visit a famous and notably mean old lady, who didn't live in a wood but who did live on a nice leafy road, in a red-brick house, where she taught singers how to sing again.

The old lady spent her days banging the underside of her jewelled fingers on to the lid of her shiny piano and glaring at her clients. One two three, two two three, three two three, and if the singers sharpened their Cs or flattened their Bs, she shook her antique walking cane in their petrified faces and threatened them with her oven.

'Come back again in a week,' the notably mean old lady said to my mother. 'There's something left. Enough to begin work.'

My mother left the old lady's parlour and, on her way out of her gate, paused for a moment to grip the ironwork. Thrilled, rejuvenated, reborn, she opened up her mouth to fill her pulsing diaphragm with fresh, winter-spiked autumnal air. But she couldn't breathe properly, couldn't fill her lungs, not in her tightly belted autumn coat. The breath that could have sailed her home, away from this graceful street, back to her modest sapling-sprinkled estate, escaped her. She had to let go of the ironwork and walk to the end of the road, like a mortal, to take the bus instead.

That night she dreamed of dancing quavers and smiling admirers. Of audiences clap-clap-clapping her again, and clasping her small fluttering hand, and looking into her sparkling green eyes to tell her that her future was halo-bright. Maybe it was during her long dream that an archangel tapped her on the shoulder and asked her to step outside for a second. He had news for her.

It turned out that I was inside her. Me. Unknown, unanticipated, unfortunate.

'Sorry about this,' the angel said, flipping through his notebook, while inside, back in the proper dream, all my mother's many admirers looked to each other in confusion, asking: 'Where has she gone? Where has the blackbird lady with the thrilling voice and the jewel-bright eyes gone? I swear she was standing right there a second ago.'

'Eh, yeah . . . sorry about this,' repeated the angel, 'but I have you down here as tasked with mothering.'

'Maybe the baby will sing,' said the diamond-crusted, notably mean old lady, shutting her piano lid with a thud, when my mother returned a week later. 'You know your own way to the door.'

The baby doesn't sing.

My father gets ready for The Club by shaving in the bathroom mirror. I watch him from my perch on the lidded toilet. He pushes out his skin from the inside with his blue tongue, to make a hard surface too, then he runs the blade over his cheek and around his chin. Scraped away, the foam reveals him, strip by strip. I push my face out from the inside with my own tongue. I'd like to shave myself visible too.

If I had been a boy, my name would have been Scott.

'That's not necessarily true,' says my mother, gluing on her false eyelashes. 'Your name could have been Nigel.'

'Lucky escape,' says my father, coming into the bedroom, his waterproof wristwatch in his hand.

'Bye bye, Nigel,' my mother says, and neither of us are sure who she's talking to.

'When they brought you in to me,' she continues, one eyelash on and one off, 'and told me you were another girl, I looked out of the window and said "Bye bye, Nigel".'

'Nigel,' I say to myself, under my tongue and behind my tonsils. I'm glad that I wasn't a Nigel.

My mother is very small. When she goes out to The Club with my father on Saturday night, people pat her on the head and say, 'Good goods come in small parcels. Is that a gin?'

She gets really really angry behind her teeth, because their big hands flatten her back-comb and she has to go all the way downstairs to the ladies' toilet to plump it up again.

'Staap patting her damn head,' says Dawn's American-non-American mother. 'She's not a freaking spaniel.'

My mother wears sable-coloured nylons and black patent-leather shoes. She stands up from the dressing-table mirror and looks warily at the wardrobe. Her false eyelashes, now firmly glued on to each eyelid, are dark and heavy; they move like caterpillars, they are alive. I wonder what would happen if I brought them in for the nature table.

My mother opens the wardrobe with her scarlet-tipped fingers, and gingerly removes the coat, her pièce de résistance.

'Madam,' I say to Norah by the lime-green hedge, whipping a hard-boiled tea towel off the washing line, 'can I interest you in this irresistible pièce de résistance, this magnificent hand-tailored, red wet-look pièce-de-résistance raincoat?'

My mother takes her brand-new coat out of the wardrobe. Her brand-new red wet-look raincoat with the thin belt around the middle. My mother had the coat made by a dressmaker to her very own specifications. The coat has been hiding underneath a shroud of brown wrapping paper since we collected it from the dressmaker. Uncovered, her brand-new coat looks startled by the pink evening light spilling in from the open bedroom curtains.

We had taken the bus into the city to collect the coat, my mother and I, walked down narrow streets, up steep linoleum-covered stairs, to the dressmaker's workshop. I waited while she tried it on, while she stood stock still in front of the dressmaker's long grey mirror.

The dressmaker had used the leftover fabric to make a red rain hat to match the coat. My mother held the hat in her hands as if it was a dead thing. She wouldn't put the hat on her head. The dressmaker had got it wrong. This was supposed to be a stupendous indoor-outdoor coat, not a fairly outrageous outdoor-outdoor coat. It should have been a coat dress, which is a dress that looks like a coat even though it's just a dress. Like my sisters' night-and-day dresses, this garment was supposed to serve many mysterious functions.

'Who is that woman?' the coat that was also a dress was supposed to make people ask. 'Who can that startling woman be?'

My mother stood dead still in front of the dressmaker's mirror.

I liked the coat; it was a friendly, cheerful coat.

'Chin up,' said the coat. 'I'll be quite useful in a light shower, you know?'

My mother was angry with the coat. This was not what she meant at all, this was not it at all.

We paid the disappointed dressmaker in crumpled money. We left. I got a comic for the bus-ride home so that my mother could concentrate on the disappointing coat.

My mother has decided to give the coat another try. She takes it out of its wrapping, puts it on over her black slip, belts it tightly. My father mutters something with his head in his sock drawer.

'I do not, I do not look like a fucking fireman,' she hisses back, her eyes bouncing off the wardrobe glass. He looks up from the drawer, cold, hard, sharp. His look extinguishes hers. His look hoses her down. He yawns, chooses thin black socks, picks up his watch from the bedside table and ties it to his wrist.

They leave in his spluttering car, tail lights sailing around the corner and out of sight.

No, you do not, madam, indeed you do not look like a fucking fireman. You look entirely individual and utterly unique.

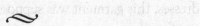

When their tail lights have absolutely unquestionably disappeared, and my parents and the nervous red coat are well on the way to The Club, I go to see which sibling is minding me. I know it's not John, because he hasn't been home since the wart row.

Louise is sitting on the floor of her bedroom in a sea of Anna's scattered clothes, painting pictures on to flat stones that she'd collected from the beach. Her poster paints are crowded on to the hearth by the unlit grate in their bedroom. Louise paints pictures on to the flat stones and then she varnishes them. When she has enough varnished stones, she will try to sell them in the Dandelion Market in the city, where the hippies go on Saturdays to buy their leather chokers and their funny brown rice and their floppy velvet hats.

'Louise, do you know any sins?'

Louise tries to do a look called withering. She doesn't do it very well. Anna can do it much better.

'Why?'

'Because I'm making my first confession soon, and we have to do actual sins.'

Louise stops painting. Instead, she starts to pull out the tiny tufty threads of her candlewick bedspread and stretch them between her small fingers. I wait for her to tell me to go away.

'Yeah, fucking children out of school and making them go to work is a sin.'

'Actually, Louise,' I want to tell her, 'it's a sin to bruise the Virgin Mary with your thoughts and deeds and language.'

I want to tell her that, but sometimes it's better to let your words pull up a seat beside your tonsils and wait.

Louise and Anna were caught by the nun chewing gum in the classroom during geography when they should have been learning about primary sources of sugar-beet production and the height of MacGillycuddy's Reeks. Louise and Anna are like twins; even though Louise is eleven months older, they were always in the same class and mostly sat beside each other. The nun said that they both had to kneel by the sides of their desks with the lumps of chewed-up gum stuck to their foreheads. They had to stay there until the gum hardened and their bare knees were etched with the grain of the parquet floor. That was just before they were expelled.

Maybe Louise would do well to consider how terribly upset the Virgin Mary was after their gum-chewing escapades.

'Were you and Anna banished like snakes?' I ask. 'Did the nun have a crozier?'

Snakes had nothing to do with anything, she says. She says there were other reasons why the nuns didn't want her and Anna to go to school any more. Reasons to do with my father not being able to find his chequebook and always being late with the fees. Louise wants to go to art college, she says, but you have to pay money to go there. Fees – for a small word, fees are very tricky. Anyway, as far as she knows, you probably need a beard and a pair of shagging Jesus sandals just to be allowed to walk through the front door of an art college. She'd have to sell a lot of painted stones before she could go to school to learn how to paint.

My mother and father met in art college. My father went there to be a painter, my mother went there for fun.

Louise looks sad and angry. I leave the room without telling her that I'll pray for her.

Anna is in the garden, smoking and squeezing out her drip-dry maxi dress with the seersucker bodice. She also says that chewing gum in class and going to hops and scooting around on the back of a Honda 50 wasn't the reason the nuns expelled them. All they ever did to deserve expulsion was eat stupid chewing gum, and roll into class late, and somehow not manage to 'have the right attitude'. She says that if everyone got expelled for chewing gum, there'd be no people left in school, including and most especially geography teachers.

'What is the right attitude?' I ask Anna.

'Paying the shagging fees,' she replies.

Anna goes out with Georgie Wilson. She sits on the

back of his motorbike, inside his spare helmet. Tonight she will wear her dress with the seersucker bodice, even though it's still wet, and a leather thong wrapped around her forehead to make her look like a hippie. The bike will splutter down the road, and the bodyguard next door, the big gentle father of all those spongy baby girls, will lift his head from bathing them in their plastic bath and antici-pate another bullet hole in the glass.

I'm going to pray for my siblings. They are exactly like the Poor Banished Children of Eve, weeping and wailing in the Valley of Tears. Except that, instead of weeping, they look straight ahead without blinking, and they do shrugging, and they bite their bottom lips and iron their curly hair and draw thick black lines over their eyelids and zip their boots up to their knees and tie-dye their T-shirts, and the PBCEs certainly didn't do any of those things. They just wailed.

When Anna and her squeezed-out, still-damp dress go off on the motorbike, tail light disappearing in the opposite direction to my parents, I go back upstairs and into John's empty bedroom.

I want to look through the binoculars that are on his windowsill, the ones that aren't really his, but borrowed from his friend Seamus for when they go birdwatching down on the marsh before the sun has even woken up. Seamus lives up the road, he has freckles and glasses and a mother with wellington boots who grows her own potatoes.

If I look through the binoculars, maybe I will see the red tail light of my parents' car just reaching the harbour, or the amber tail light of the spluttering motorbike taking

Anna somewhere I can't go. All I can see, though, are the saplings stretching out on each side of the long pale road and, straight opposite our house, Celine O'Flaherty's bedroom curtains drawn tight.

I sit on the Tintawn carpet. Tintawn is kind of a carpet and kind of not; it's made of thickened string. 'Grosgrain and Ribgrass,' says the half-peeled sticker near the door. 'Practical and hard-wearing.' The carpet is a remnant; there was barely enough to cover the box-room floor. Remnant means a bit that's left over, a bit that is not that much use to anyone.

If you turn the binoculars around and look through the bigger circles, the thickened glass circles at the other end, everything looks really far away, instead of really close up. Far away but perfectly clear, as if you are seeing things for the first time, like a scientist, or an explorer, or someone watching from a different planet. I turn the binoculars backwards and scan John's room through the big circles.

On John's floor, there is the portable turntable that he shares with my sisters: bright red lid, shiny gold clasps. There is a Beatles album on the floor next to it. *Revolver.* The Beatles' faces drawn in long black pen on the cover. My brother can draw just like that. I focus the glass on the album cover. The four Beatles are thickly inked. I have to remember to like John Lennon the best if I'm going to be cool, but even from this immense, alien distance, I prefer Paul McCartney.

I swing my binoculared head, see my brother's bird book beside his bed, open on Brent geese. Under the bed there are tiny little cigarette butts in a jam-jar lid, hand-rolled butts so small they could fit a doll's lips. His skullcap is under there too. The skullcap looks as frightening as its name. Under the scrutiny of the backward glass, it looks like a person, like the bandaged man who could rise up from the quicksand and grasp your ankles and drag you down there with him. I know what the skullcap is. John told me that it is something you wear when you're playing rugby, for protection. We were talking under the dining-room table, and John said he should never take the fucking thing off. I said a silent prayer for him, diverted the arrow that was heading straight for the Virgin Mary's ribcage.

John was made the captain of his rugby team last year, but we never went to see him play, and anyway he's stopped being the captain now, so it's too late. There is a leather jacket that I've never seen before on the back of John's chair, and next to it, on the floor beside the chair, there is his school bag. Inside, there are ink stains and a sandwich wrapped in parchment paper. I open the paper, keeping the binoculars to my eyes, and look: the bread is green, the mould moves like bubbling soup. The sandwich died a long time ago, unnoticed. Everyone just got on with their very important alien business, regardless of the ageing bread.

I taste bacon rind in my mouth. I think that John was telling me the truth when he said he is my father's son. I am not one hundred per cent sure about my sisters yet, but I think John was telling the truth about that too. I'm going to have to ask someone even if my ruddy head gets sliced off.

There is no wart on my father's palm. I checked while he was lighting a cigarette after breakfast the next day. Palm. I like that word. I don't know anybody with warts.

On Monday, I will bring in a penny for the black babies, as instructed by Sister Most Immaculate, and I'll ask Norah if she knows anybody with warts. Especially someone with warts on their palm. Norah's very good on illness and diseases. Several people Norah and I know have got verrucas, but not warts. You get verrucas from swimming lessons, but nobody in our house ever went to a swimming lesson.

God should have stayed where he was, put his feet up and left that leftover rib well enough alone, because Eve turned out to be unrepentant. A bad apple. God gave Eve a dress made of fig leaves and butterflies, and told her, specifically, not to eat a particular apple that would soon be offered to her by a talking snake. However, Eve chose to use her free will instead, utterly ignoring God's instructions. And when the aforementioned snake turned up, offering her the apple, which was neatly tucked into its coils, she said, 'Oh, cool, thanks a million!', and flicked her long blonde hair over her shoulder, and bit. Bit hard.

And from that very moment, from that very second, the world, which was barely used, barely even touched, the world, which still had its plastic wrapping on it, the brand-new world, which had only ever had one careful owner, was filled with plague and pestilence and dirt and pain. And all Eve's banished children, children that she didn't even know she had, came screaming and howling out of dank caves and holes in the ground and lakes of quicksand, and started running around like lunatics.

Lunatics! Sending up their sighs, mourning and weeping in a vale of tears. And what did Eve do? Eve lay in the bath, locusts swarming, combing her long yellow hair with a hedgehog while her little dog yapped at the door.

'And tell me, what magnificent contribution do you plan on making to this world, E-E-E-Eve?' said God quietly, quietly, quietly, pushing down his cuticles with his metal ruler (which is never a good sign).

'M-M-M-Me?' asked Eve, through a mouthful of crunchy apple. 'I fhought I might be a hair ostess, or maybe a continuity hannouncer.'

'Don't speak with your mouth full,' said God. 'And breathe through your nose when you're chewing!'

'I said,' said Eve, swallowing the yellow flesh, 'I said I thought I might be an air hostess or maybe a continuity announcer.'

'You thought what??' said God. 'You thought what???'

And thunder rolled, and lightning struck, and the saplings withered, and the floods came rushing down the mountain, and the whole Earth fell into a big hole right in the middle of itself. And that was the last that Eve saw of that particular garden.

Everybody is gone too far, tail lights flashing. I return the borrowed binoculars to the windowsill. Soon Louise's Protestant boyfriend will turn up in his souped-up Mini car and his T-shirt that says 'Happiness is a Tight Pussy' on it. Then I will have to go to bed with the radio. It's quite a nice T-shirt; it has a picture of a kitten in a champagne glass on the front and the words written underneath. In the morning I will go into my parents' bedroom, quietly, to see if the caterpillars are still on my mother's eyes and to ask the red coat if it made any friends.

5

Druids and Numbs

FIRST CONFESSION AND HOLY COMMUNION ARE A breath away. Brown envelopes with little peek-a-boo windows and the words FINAL DEMAND stamped on them in nice pink letters are all over the kitchen table next to my religion copybook with the soothing blank pages on which I am to draw Jesus dying for our sins.

It is twenty past five. My siblings aren't home; my father is not home, not even nearly home. All the way up and down the road the husbands are getting out of their black Morris Minors and pale-green Cortinas and inspecting their budding roses while they finger their keys. In a minute their wives will open their front doors, rubbing their hands on their aprons, pushing back their perms, and the husbands will hand over their newspapers and maybe their empty flasks and ask if there's any sign of that bloody window cleaner at all at all.

It is teatime on our road, but we have our dinner at teatime, and a car that brings my father home in the dark. My mother and I are having spaghetti for dinner, again, which is fine by me. I only eat spaghetti and fish fingers and baby beetroot and picnic salmon from a tin. It's simpler that way.

'Christ on a fucking stick,' says my mother to all the bills, which is quite funny, because she sounds exactly like my father. I'm not sure what kind of stick they mean; maybe they mean Christ on a pogo stick. I'm drawing Jesus on a crucifix, which is two sticks. Some of my spaghetti has fallen off my plate and it's curling around the word DEMAND, making it look much prettier.

My mother puts down her fork, rubs her hands over her eyes, and her eyebrows disappear. They swirl away like muddy potato water going down the sink, and just then the front doorbell rings.

She jumps out of her chair and rushes to open it, quickly checking her reflection in the sunburst mirror. Maybe she thinks it's the egg man, maybe she'd like an egg, but it's not the egg man. Maybe she thinks it is my brother, but it's not my brother, or my sisters. There, standing on the doorstep, is the tall bank manager with the long beige face, and now he's wearing a long beige coat to match it.

He is standing on the porch with his head tilted to one side, looking awfully disappointed by my mother's watery, browless face and her naked, very surprised mouth.

'I'm terribly sorry, so terribly sorry, so terribly sorry for disturbing you at this time,' he says. Maybe he's terribly sorry for disturbing our spaghetti, but I don't think so.

'It's spaghetti,' I tell him. 'We're having spaghetti for dinner.' But he can't see me behind my fork.

And now my mother has to take a deep breath and pretend to be bright and gay and utterly lovely, even without her eyebrows, even without having had time to colour herself in.

The bank manager is looking terribly worried.

It's funny to see him on our doorstep. I don't really recognize him standing up. Usually we have an appointment to see him. Usually we flitter down to the bank when my mother has her beauty spot on right, and when he is sitting behind his desk, where there is a pen that is tied to a holder by a little brassy chain. Maybe that's to stop people putting it in their pocket and forgetting all about it. Usually he does tutting and smiling.

'Oh, that!' my mother is saying on the doorstep, although the bank manager hasn't quite finished his very long sentence. 'My husband will have that sorted out by Monday. A blip! Just a blip!'

She can laugh like splintered glass or like warm bubbling water; both are in her repertoire. Having a repertoire is like having different outfits to hang on your voice. Today she chooses the splintered laugh.

The last time we flittered down to the bank, all coloured in and eyebrowed, my mother was wearing a black-and-white tweed cape that her friend Cora made her. Cora lives on our road. She is an artist too, she paints pictures at her kitchen table, and she also makes capes for ladies, and crocheted hats to match. She does this for money.

'Paint!' my mother says to her over their teacups. 'For God's sake.'

'Money,' Cora says. 'I've got to make money.'

Cora makes and sells the pretty capes and hats because her husband doesn't like sharing, and because she has three children to feed. I like when we go up the road to visit Cora. Sometimes Cora minds me when my mother goes down the country in Ed's square car to sing to the lame and the mad who don't live in Dublin. I watch Cora stand on her kitchen stoop and fold her bony brown arms over her apron. She closes her eyes because the sun is shining on her, and then she remembers something and straightens up and looks frightened at the clock, to see how much time is left before her husband comes home.

Cora has three boys and two rabbits and three Manx cats and a rockery. But mainly she has the husband that growls like an actual dog. I like playing cars with her boys.

Cora made a beautiful crocheted button for the neck of my mother's cape, which my mother unfastened when we entered the cool, grey bank for our appointment with the bank manager, the same bank manager who is now standing in our porch. She held her black leather gloves in her hands. Her fingernails were like oval cherries; they were the same colour as her mouth.

We were asked to wait, so we did. We waited by the tall counter, and my mother put one of her gloves down on the countertop. Her arm was hidden under the loose cape, and when the long beige bank manager came out of his office to greet her, his lip quivered like he was going to cry. He looked all upset like he hadn't done his homework properly, like he'd only done the writing-down bits and never learned his Irish spellings. I don't know why he was upset.

We stood by the countertop, my mother talking quietly through her cherry lips. The bank manager had tiny silvery tears in the corners of his pale-blue eyes. He began nodding slowly. He began, too, to gently pat my mother's leather glove on the counter, and then to stroke it, each fragile touch loosening the strings on his awfully big purse. My mother, pleased by his nodding acquiescence to her fragile demands, looked down and noticed the brave strokes her little glove was receiving, noticed his trembling fingers. She tried to slip her hand inside the shell of the glove. Talking, talking, talking all the time, gaily laughing like bubbling water, so the bank manager wouldn't notice that his attention had been spent on empty leather.

'Forgive me,' she says to the perplexed-looking bank manager, standing now on our doorstep at spaghetti time, standing on our doorstep out of office hours, looking like a long disappointed drink of water.

'Forgive me,' she says to his flat beige face, a face clearly wondering where the cherry-lipped cape lady has disappeared to, wondering if, indeed, he has imagined her.

'Forgive me,' says my mother. 'My eyebrows . . . I must look like a rabbit.'

When we get back to the table the spaghetti is cold and the paperwork is sick and tired of shouting.

THERE IS A GIRL ON NORAH'S ROAD WHO HAS A NANNY. A nanny is someone who minds you. The nanny is a grown-up girl with a long shiny ponytail and nice brown eyes, and her name is Majella. Majella cleans the house and minds the two sausage dogs and the one little girl who lives in it. The little girl is called Mary, which must be pretty boring for her.

When I go to Norah's house we sometimes walk down the road and ask Mary to come out and play, but she doesn't. She never comes out to play because Majella brushes Mary's hair one hundred times every day and she doesn't want her to mess it up.

One day Norah and I are on an expedition up and down her road to see if anyone has put the Child of Prague out. It has been raining for quite some time, and we are blue in the face praying for a fine day for the communion, as we have been instructed to do by Sister Mary Immaculately Immaculate, Sister Clean-under-the-Bed. There is a lady on my road who puts a little statue of the Child of Prague in her front garden when she wants the sun to shine on her dahlias. But she hasn't had her statue out for ages, so we're hoping to see if there are any other ones out and about. I'm not a hundred per cent sure who the Child of Prague is, or what special prayers he says to the sun. Maybe he and Jesus are pen pals.

I'm not very hopeful that the Child of Prague (who, even though he is supposed to be a very holy little boy, has a crown and lipstick and a fur coat and a mean expression) can do much about the banks of clouds that stretch right over every single bit of sky that we can see. Anyway, the Child of Prague isn't out in any of the gardens on Norah's road either, but Mary is. While nanny Majella is washing sausage-dog pee off the kitchen floor, Mary has wandered out to her front garden and is standing still behind some kind of fairy-tale wooden fence, which has wet pink roses growing in, around and up and over it, so it is difficult to see her properly or to find a good talking place.

'Why do you have that wood on top of your garden wall

anyway?' we ask Mary, and Mary says it is for privacy, that some people like to enjoy their privacy in private.

'It's called rustic,' she says, and we are impressed.

'Do you have a Child of Prague you could bring out to your garden?' we ask. But she says their Child of Prague has to stay on the window ledge on the landing, looking out over her garage, that he isn't allowed out.

'I have a nanny,' she says, just as we are about to walk away.

'Do you think it will stop raining?' I ask Mary, because people on our road always talk about the weather and I'm not sure yet what a nanny is.

'My nanny's name is Majella and she had a baby boy,' says Mary. 'He was taken away from her as soon as he came out of her bottom.'

This is a shock, on many levels.

'What was his name?' Norah asks.

'Ringo,' she replies, but I think she is making that bit up.

Apparently Majella's baby, the fruit in her womb, had to go to an orphanage because there was no Joseph around, and no archangel either. Majella is nice enough, Mary says, sometimes she'll give you a biscuit but sometimes she'll pinch. She isn't a saint, Mary says. Not that we have asked if she is. For someone who doesn't usually do talking or playing, Mary has a lot to say for herself. She says that Majella's baby was put into the orphanage until it could go to a deserving Catholic family with a proper mammy and a daddy and a proper back garden. And that Majella was lucky to find a fresh start and a position in her parents' box bedroom.

When Mary has finished her long story she folds her arms and looks at us through the rustic fence. Two armadillo spiders are heading out on a long journey to find their missing family, making awfully good progress along the fallen wet petals.

'You have lovely hair, Mary,' I say, because I'm not exactly sure if this is all good news or bad news, or if I should be happy for Majella or sad for Majella. Also, Norah and I aren't used to Mary telling us secrets.

I'm good at secrets. I keep them in a room inside my head that has a brass key. Like the piano key. Now I am going to have to make more space. I don't even tell Norah the 'who we didn't see today' secret.

I don't think Majella is lucky. She had to give her baby to the orphanage; that's not lucky at all. The little match girl was in an orphanage, and she ended up dead in the snow with blackened matches all around her frozen feet. And Oliver was in an orphanage, and he had gruel once a day and a dead mother underneath a willow tree.

'I think Majella should take her baby back from the deserving Catholics and their stupid garden,' I tell Norah.

'I think Majella should kill the people who took her baby with an axe, and then bury them in quicksand,' Norah replies thoughtfully.

I am standing on a chair feeding Lucky, our budgerigar. I am feeding him dandelion leaves through the narrow bars of his cage, which stands in a corner of our kitchen next to the stiff Polyester kitchen curtains, which are all the rage.

The pale-brown envelopes with the pink writing are

still all over the kitchen table. My mother is looking and looking and looking at the words FINAL DEMAND to see if it will change into something else. Sometimes party invitations have pale-pink writing on them, but they usually have balloons as well.

Lucky the budgie is flapping around and around his cage, banging his little turquoise head off the bars in sheer happiness. Dandelion time is his absolute favourite time of the day.

'You're going to poison him,' my mother mutters, trying to do adding up in her head, which never works for me.

Lucky isn't always so lively. Before I had the very good idea of feeding him dandelion leaves, he would spend practically the whole day sitting on his swing. Hour after hour after hour, occasionally pecking at his own glum face in his little hanging mirror. Peck, peck, peck, all through *Farmers' Weekly* and two Radio Éireann weather forecasts.

'I suspect that bird may be clinically depressed,' says my father, coming into the kitchen in his sailing trousers, car keys in his hand, sword swinging overhead.

While Lucky headbutts the bars, my father exhales slowly, gently fumigating Lucky's cage with a blast of Sweet Afton.

'*He's* depressed?' my mother shoots back, fists full of final demands. '*He's* depressed? *I'm bloody* depressed.'

Lucky, worn out with excitement, flaps back to his perch and tries to find his own reflection through the smoke.

'Perhaps,' says my father to the dazed bird, 'Lucky may not have been the most apt of monikers. Eh?'

'There's a girl called Mary who lives on Norah's road who has a nanny, and the nanny had a baby, and then her baby was taken away and put in an orphanage,' I tell my father.

The words just pop out, even though they are supposed to be under lock and key in my secrets box. I want to look inside my own mouth and ask it what the hell it thinks it is doing, blurting things out, forgetting to be careful.

'What baby?' asks my mother. 'What are you talking about?'

'Fucking druids,' says my father. 'Druids and numbs.'

Druids and numbs are what he calls priests and nuns.

OUR FIRST HOLY COMMUNION WILL BE THE MOST IMportant day of our lives.

'Thus far,' says Norah, who has decided to collect her baby teeth in a money box and important expressions in her mind.

'The most' – breath – 'important' – breath – 'day' – breath – 'thus far.'

'That's a lively wheeze, Norhannah,' says Sister Immaculate, whipping out her notebook and writing down 'lively wheeze', just in case she hasn't enough to worry about.

I don't want to bruise the Virgin Mary unnecessarily, I don't want to add to her anguish, but I don't actually like Sister Immaculate. I miss Sister Celestine and her talk about all the mysterious sorrows and the pain of this temporal world, and how magical it will be for us in the kingdom of heaven when we're dead. Sister Immaculate is not interested in banished children, and plagues of locusts, and wailing and weeping in the valley of tears;

she's interested in threes going into nines and twos going into tens.

My numbers don't want to go into anything, they just want to skate over my copybook and land in a huddle in the corner looking for their shoes.

We see Sister Celestine at lunchtime when we go to the lunch room for our soup. She sits at the long refectory table staring at her bread roll, shoved up next to Sister Alphonsus, who has keys jangling from a rope around her habit, and small round glasses, and huge cheeks full of iced caramels.

Four Sister Celestines would go into one Sister Alphonsus, easily. That's maths.

We are learning new prayers from Sister Immaculate in preparation for our First Holy Communion. Some of these prayers are for the attention of the Holy Ghost, also known as the Holy Spirit, who is a kind of odd-job man for Jesus and will be clearing a path for him to enter our souls.

The-Holy-Ghost-also-known-as-the-Holy-Spirit lives with Mary, Earth mother of Jesus, and Joseph the carpenter, who she married when Jesus was still fruit in her womb.

The Holy Spirit is quite complicated to explain because, although he is a fully fledged member of the Holy Family, he isn't really a person. He has wings. Also, he's harder to get to know, because he's out of town quite a lot, on important business to do with the Pope. It's probably most useful to think of the Holy Spirit more like a pet. A beloved, important pet, a kind of Holy Budgie, only bigger and holier.

Before we can even think about Holy Lovely Communion we have to make our First Terrifying Confession. Norah says that we really need to start committing some sins soon, so that we have something to tell the priest about when we do it.

'Have you thought of any sins yet?' I ask her, on the way back out to the yard after lunch room.

'Oh yep,' she says, putting her hands into the pockets of her grey pinafore and emptying out nuggets of butter pats wrapped up in gold foil. 'I'm doing stealing.'

I hold one of the butter pats, softening already in my palm. I clutch it harder, hoping some of its useful sinfulness will rub off on me.

'The lamb of God takes away the sins of the world. Happy are those who are called to his supper.' Ding-a-ling-a-ling.

We spend the mornings now in the wooden pews of the convent chapel, practising for confession and communion. It is my favourite place.

I still can't knit or purl. I can't cast off or on. I can't add, subtract, multiply or divide. I can't spell. Sister Immaculate itches with annoyance when she sees my stupid face. She is not allowed to hit us, because of our fathers' cheques (as soon as they can find their chequebooks), but I can see underneath her glasses that she wants to knock me into the middle of next week.

My biggest problem is Irish, which we learn every day for hours and hours and hours, and which is a plateful of terror. Irish is everywhere, hidden in the copybook cupboards, sniggering under the desks, jumping up and down on the blackboard. We mice have to swallow down the language whole. It sticks in my throat like hard, cold potatoes. I can't swallow the language down, there are edges all over the words that make them fall back out of my mouth and on to my desk.

I am weak. Our school reports come in the post, land on the mat next to the final demands, next to the cross letters from Arnotts, my mother's favourite department store, and the mean letters from the Electricity Supply Board and the outraged letters from the taxman, who always puts a picture of a harp on his envelopes, and the quietly furious handwritten letters from the nuns, saying: 'Have you not found your ruddy chequebook yet?'

'She's weak,' the reports say, in the nuns' perfect joined-up writing. 'Weak, weak, weak, weak, weak.'

My father puts them in the kitchen fire, along with anything else my mother doesn't get to first.

My father hates the Irish language, every *buailte* and *fada*, and he haaates all the druids who taught it. In his school, in Limerick, which is a city he never visits and rarely ever mentions, they had to learn Latin and Greek through Irish. If you got your homework wrong in my father's school, the priests swished their soutanes like matadors and headed boldly in your direction. When they landed in front of your desk, they grabbed you by the hair and flipped you over with a sharp kick of their polished brogues, and then they held you out the high-up classroom window by your ankles, so that you could see the ground floating above your upside-down head. And you could feel your kneesocks slipping through their nicotine-stained fingers, and just when you thought that you were about to slip from their delicate grasp, they'd hoist you back in, your stomach now in your pants, and say: 'Last chance, boy, last chance.'

Only the priests in Limerick didn't do that to my father, because he was tall and fast, and he played on the wing, and his father was a Protestant who might know something they didn't know, and because even then my father could slowly inhale his untipped cigarettes and look the priests right in the eye. He was more than six feet long; they were probably afraid that they would drop him and lose the cup match. They only really held the small boys with the big mistakes in their copybooks out of the window.

When he remembers this, my father breathes in and out through his nose, like a boxer or an impatient pony, or like when we are in the soupy air of his mother's nursing-home bedroom.

'She is weak, very weak, very very weak,' the nuns remind my mother when she picks me up at the convent door. 'Weak, weak, weak, weak, weak. Weak weak weak weak weak.'

I'm good at praying, though, and I can draw. That's why I like the chapel. There are silver stars painted on the domed ceiling, and the room is full of plaster saints. Some saints have doves at their feet, and there are lots of baby Jesuses on plinths, and several types of Marys in a variety of plaster robes. There is Mass every day, for the older girls and for the nuns. We are allowed to watch and do the standing-up and the sitting-down bits, but we won't be doing the best part, walking like water bearers up to the altar, with our hands joined, and receiving Jesus on our tongues, until after our big day.

Everyone has to bow their heads when the bell rings. No one is allowed to look up when the priest opens the tabernacle door, because that is where Jesus lives, and the light hurts his eyes. If the tabernacle door is left open too long, tiny little bits of him can seep out and turn to dust. I try not to, but I look, under my eyelashes, which might actually be a mortal sin (mortal sins are ten times worse than ordinary sins). I think I might have seen his tiny shoulder.

This is a practice run, but at real communion, at actual First Holy Communion, the priest will turn the body of Christ into bread, and the blood of Christ into wine, and he will drink the wine from a big gold chalice, and we will eat a tiny portion of God, made into a wafer.

'I wouldn't be very happy to be called to his supper,' says Norah.

'I wouldn't' – breath – 'be very happy' – breath – 'to be called' – breath – 'to his supper.'

We are in the yard, leaning against the red-bricked convent wall, the butter long melted between our hot fingers. The polish fumes in the convent chapel make it harder for Norah to breathe. Every morning the quiet women in the crossover aprons, who work in the convent, polish the floors with big hoovers that look like robots. God bless the work Mary/Mona/Bridget/Other Mary, the nuns say, when we troop into the chapel in our indoor shoes, disturbing their ministrations.

While Norah and I wait for her breath train to come, we lean against the wall watching Claudette jump-skip. Two other mice twirl the rope for her. Claudette is the best skipper in our class, arms pinned to her grey sides, corkscrew curls shooting out of her head, her pleated skirt lifting like a song:

> *Vote, vote, vote for de Valera!*
> *In comes Deirdre at the door-i-o.*
> *Deirdre is the one who will have a bit of fun*
> *And we don't want Claudette any more-i-o.*

The trick in this game is to run in when your name is sung, and pick up on the rhythm of the rope. My feet are cautious; they don't like the challenge. They don't want to be the ones to break the game. I hang back with Norah; her breath is still pulling at her, badgering her, blocking her path. She leans forward, hands on her knees, slows down the fizzy exhalations, makes her mouth round as a whistle. Breathe out, breathe in, breathe in, breathe out.

'What would the lamb of God have for his supper anyway?' I ask.

'Grass,' says Norah, 'and hay.'

'I don't want to go then, not for grass.'

Norah has taken another puff of her inhaler, even though she's not supposed to take it twice. The blue colour leaves her lips; she can breathe again.

'Supper is ready!' she shouts, starting to run.

'Supper is ready!' I shout, running after her.

And now we are the Virgin Marys, wiping our hands on our plaster aprons and calling out the kitchen window. And we are all the hungry Apostles, running around Bethlehem, washing our hands in the donkey trough.

'Hurry up, Jesus!' we shout. 'It'll be stone cold.'

And Jesus stops washing his soul in the baptismal font, and runs after us, and we are free and we are fast and we are happy. And when we get to Mary's kitchen, a baby angel slips inside and dilutes the MiWadi, and Mary says: 'For God's sake, will you all sit down! Didn't I tell you five minutes ago your supper was on the table!' And we all sit down at God's Formica-topped table, me and Norah, and Jesus, and the Apostles, and some pre-cured lepers (who are dead grateful to have hands to eat with), and some scribes and Pharisees (who were only invited at the last minute), and some shepherds and fishermen and carpenters, and some blind children who can see, and some cripples who can walk, and a couple of children who fell into a shallow river at the back of the shops and got polio, who Jesus cured without even having to look up from his homework, and some cattle and some sheep and several donkeys and one sleepy camel. And everyone sits down to a massive dinner of grass and grapes and loaves and fish fingers and beetroot, and the food stays on the plates, every morsel, and doesn't sail through the air like Russian ballerinas.

MY WHITE COMMUNION DRESS IS HANGING IN MY mother's wardrobe, and in a paper bag, on her dressing table, there are my white gloves and white kneesocks and a white velvet hairband that she will sew my short white net veil on to. I have a small white drawstring cotton bag, in case people give me sweets or money, and I have new white sandals, and I even have a new white vest and new white pants. We went into Arnotts, which is the big big department store in the city; we paid for them with my mother's Arnotts card, which is a kind of magic card.

'Whoops,' said my mother when the bill came through the door.

My mother says my dress is tasteful, simple. Simple can be a good word. But simple can also be an unkind word.

'Simple,' says Claudette when one of the boys in our class doesn't make it to the toilet on time when we are waiting in our classroom, fingers on our lips, to hop the tiles to the convent chapel for our First Confession practice. The boy pees on the parquet floor, water coming out of his trousers and his eyes. Sister Immaculate looks like she is going to faint.

'Simple,' Claudette whispers, making her finger-on-the-lips finger go around and around at the side of her head, to show that the boy is a crazy person.

Claudette is kind of my friend and kind of not my friend. Sometimes she is a bit mean. She is also interesting, though, and she's a unique dancer. Claudette uses her free will in ballet class, even though we're not supposed to. We've been doing a lot of free will in school; apparently, it can be quite dangerous. It's inside all of us, Sister Immaculately Immaculate says, and it needs to be curbed, whatever that is.

Claudette dances around and around the auditorium in her red ballet shoes, waving her pom-pom sticks around and around her curly head, only listening to her free will and with scant regard for the rest of us.

'You have scant regard for the rest of us, Claudette,' says our dancing teacher, Miss McAnally, and she closes her eyes in despair. 'I'm closing my eyes in despair,

Claudette,' she says, but Claudette's free will doesn't pay her the slightest bit of attention. Miss McAnally comes to the school twice a week with her pianist, a tiny little woman who never takes her coat off and is even older than the piano. She has two hearing aids in her big grey doughy ears, and I think she likes Claudette. She keeps playing and playing, and smiling and smiling, even when Miss McAnally tells her to 'Stop!', and Claudette keeps dancing and dancing, and then Miss McAnally closes her emerald-green eyeshadow eyes and tries to breathe in and out through her little nose.

Deep lines radiate out from the corners of Miss McAnally's eyes like runaway trains. And when she dips her head while she's teaching us to curtsey ('bend and bow, bend and bow'), we can see the ice-white line of her scalp running through the middle of her blue-black hair. Her hair sits in round nests on either side of her head, coiled into hard black buns. If she uncoiled her buns, her hair would reach the floor. Norah says that the old pianist lady is Miss McAnally's mother, and that they live together in a cottage with a black cat and a cauldron. She says that, sooner or later, Claudette will end up in their oven.

I like dancing, but I'm weak at dancing as well. I keep forgetting which is my left and which is my right. I'd like to do Claudette's kind of dancing, dancing with your arms and your legs instead of your left and right. Dancing with your eyes shut and the whole room to move around in, but we're not allowed to do that.

After ballet class, at little break, Claudette describes her communion dress to us. It is floor-length, she says, and made from taffeta and silk and Crimplene and lace. She is going to have a fur stole over her shoulders, and a tiara on her head, and lipstick on her mouth, and the night before the big day she will go to bed with her hair tied up in rags so that in the morning her curly curls will fall on to her shoulders in long looping ringlets.

'And,' she says, 'wait for it . . .' And we wait, Marietta biscuits and banana sandwiches suspended in mid-air. 'I'll be wearing silver slingback shoes over my anklesocks.'

Silver slingbacks! The rest of us might as well turn up barefoot.

I am upstairs sitting on the carpeted floor, outside the locked bathroom door. My mother is behind the door, in the bath. I am sitting on the carpet listening to her sing. This is a red-letter day; today we are going to buy my communion coat.

The carpet is blue with a black design. I try to sit on just the blue bits, but it is impossible. The carpet looks like an earthquake, like when the Earth cracks and the black space underneath opens up. If you fell into one of those cracks, you could fall for ever and ever until you came to hell.

My mother sings quietly; she sings that it's life's illusions she recalls and that she really doesn't know life at all. She sings that there were so many things she would have done, but clouds got in her way. I like this moons-and-dunes song, even though it's really sad.

If you absolutely make yourself stop imagining falling into hell through the carpet, and look long enough at the blue bits, you can imagine instead that you are sitting on a tiny black island in the middle of the sea. The carpet is ocean-blue, but the ocean I know, the ocean that crashes into the harbour wall and pours down on the fish boxes, the ocean that leaps up on to the long pier where my father and I walk to The Club, hand in hand, that ocean is green. It is green and deep, and thick as soup, and sometimes it's gunmetal grey.

I am usually afraid of the water, but sometimes, when we go to the seafront hotel, my father takes me with him into the long turquoise swimming pool, and then I am no longer afraid. I sit on his back and he is a dolphin, head down in the glistening water, white back curled over. The snowdrift lady, the 'so-that's-who-you-are' lady, sits on the side of the pool, stirring the water with her painted toenails.

'Magnificent,' she says when he emerges to take a breath. 'Magnificent.'

I'm waiting for my mother to get out of the bath because any minute now we are actually going to miss the bus into town, where we have our very important business to attend to. First Holy Communion business.

'Claudette is wearing silver slingbacks,' I call through the door to my bathing mother. 'Silver slingbacks and an actual tiara!'

I hear her getting out of the bath.

The bus will jettison us on Middle Abbey Street, outside Uncle George's Pet Shop (jettison is a word borrowed from Norah's expression collection – it means something like drop). I like Uncle George's Pet Shop. I like it as long as I remember not to look too closely at the mice. Mice make me feel ill, even though they are just small furry things with tails.

Once Louise and Anna saw a mouse in our kitchen when my parents were out at a swimming-pool party. (They hadn't intended to go to a swimming-pool party, my mother explained the next morning when I went in to wake her, and her eye make-up was streaked down her face, and her eyelashes had walked halfway down her cheeks, and the whole room smelt like beer and chlorine. They'd gone to The Club for a couple of drinks and ended up in a floodlit pool with somebody famous and some other not-so-famous but very jolly people. 'But you had no togs,' I reminded her. 'We wrapped ourselves in towels,' she replied.) Louise and Anna went to bed with a big sign on their door saying 'Mouse in the House. Do Not Open This Door'. And when my father came back from the party, he wrote a note from the mouse, saying that he thought it best to move on as he hadn't been much of a hit. He also drew a picture of a little mouse on the notice. The mouse was at the bus stop with his suitcase in his mousey hand and a sad expression. Everyone was pretty happy then. Mice have their uses.

Uncle George's Pet Shop is where we usually go to buy Lucky the budgerigar the lumps of chalky stone that he uses to sharpen his beak on. We put the stone through the bars of his cage and hope for the best, hope that it's enough to take his mind off his dreadful life.

'Christ, what a dreadful life,' my mother often says, standing in front of Lucky's cage, watching him beat his wings off the bars. She bought him his hanging mirror in Uncle George's shop, so that he wouldn't feel so alone. But when she first hung it in his cage, his beady black eyes shot out on stalks and he flew at it and pecked and pecked at his reflection. In horror.

'Is he kissing himself?' Anna asked from sideways. Her head was on the ironing board, cheek down. Louise was laying brown wrapping paper over Anna's flattened-out hair, and then she was going to iron it, poker-straight.

'No,' said Louise. 'He's not kissing himself. He's trying to kill himself.'

'What's Lucky for?' I asked my mother one day. 'Why do we have him? Why does he live in a cage in our kitchen?'

'For?' she asked, as if she'd never heard the word before. 'For? He's not *for* anything. He's purely decorative.'

When my mother has leftover pastry, she rolls it out again and cuts it into the shape of leaves with the paring knife. Then she brushes the cold flat leaves with beaten egg, to make them shine, and then she sticks the leaves on to the unbaked tart.

'What are the leaves for?' I ask.

'Why does everything have to be *for* something?' she asks. 'Some things just *are*.'

'Are the pastry leaves purely decorative?' I ask.

'Decorative and edible,' she replies.

My mother likes decorative things. She likes beauty spots and pillar-box-red fingernails. She likes the hand-painted maracas that she uses to beat out the time until something interesting happens. Lucky and my mother spend a lot of time in front of the mirror waiting to see what will happen next. Lucky, who should have been a purely decorative thing, is also a depressed thing and, to be perfectly honest, sometimes a little bit of a scary

thing. But I suppose sometimes things don't go according
to plan.

My communion-coat-buying day, which I've been really
really really looking forward to, has been thwarted – along
with all my other great Holy Communion plans – by
worry and difficulty. (Thwarted is another one of Norah's
important words.)

My main worry is sin. There I am in town, with my
mother, to buy a coat to wear over my communion dress,
and yet I still haven't committed a single good sin. Not
one proper sin, and there are only days to go until our first
confession. What is the point in a brand-new coat, to put
over your brand-new dress, if your soul can't be cleaned
brand-new because you haven't managed to sully it in the
first place?

I am weak. The nuns are right. A failure. With nothing
worth confessing. Norah says you have to be on the
lookout for sinning opportunities. You have to be smart
to do really good sins. I am trying to be on the lookout for
sinning opportunities, but where are they? Unless I was
to release Uncle George's sleeping snakes on to Middle
Abbey Street, I can't envisage much sinning scope there,
and the bus ride into town is certainly not a sinning
opportunity, it is a pleasant experience.

We sit quietly upstairs and gently breathe in other
people's cigarette smoke. My mother hums her bathtub
song softly and tunefully, and I look out the window at
the tops of the trees, which is not a sight you see every
day.

As I listen, looking at the tops of the doll-pink apple

blossoms, I think about the clouds that got in the way of the so many things that my mother would have done if the clouds *hadn't* got in her way. I make a list of the clouds that got in her way, some puffy, some black. The problem, though, is that thinking about my mother's cloudy sky doesn't help me get on with any actual sinning.

CLOUD ONE: WHEN MY MOTHER WAS A LITTLE GIRL SHE had a dog called Hector, and she also had a sister with lovely teeth and glossy hair and nice brown skin, and a brother with similar attributes. My mother was the youngest in the family, and from the black-and-white photographs that lie in a heap in the bottom of her old desk drawer, she looked like a happy little girl. She also looked quite bold. Bold means daring and adventurous if you live in England; if you live in Ireland it means that you don't do what you're told, and that sooner or later you will run into serious trouble. Consequences.

The photograph I like best is the one where she is sitting on Hector's back. Hector looks a little bit embarrassed. Hector looks like he is wondering if he should tell her that he's not actually a horse, or indeed a small pony, but a very busy Jack Russell with sharp, intelligent ears and a lot of important digging to do. I think Hector must have kept his counsel because my mother looks perfectly at home on Hector's narrow back.

The old desk where the photographs of my mother are kept is in our living room now. It used to belong to my grandfather, Nathaniel, who was the father of my mother and her two handsome siblings. The desk used to live in the pretty house my mother grew up in, with her family, which, as well as her siblings, also included my grandfather, my grandmother Madeleine, and their maid, Nelly. Nelly looked after things because Madeleine, pleasant as she was, was also quite forgetful.

Madeleine married Nathaniel because her sister, who was his intended (intended means someone you intended to spend your whole and entire life with), died. She just sneezed and died, which people often did in the olden days, Norah says. Nathaniel was at a bit of a loss, but he liked Madeleine just as much as her dead sister, and so they got married instead. After their three babies were born, my grandmother drifted off into the long back garden to grow dahlias. Big red dahlias with earwigs scuttling out of the petals. Thank goodness for Nelly, the maid in the scullery, because someone had to peel the potatoes and remember when it was time for dinner. Someone needed to keep in mind that my grandfather would soon be returning from Dublin Castle, where he worked as a civil servant, doing important tasks to keep the island afloat. If Maddie was left in charge there'd be pansies and foxgloves for tea, and nectar drunk from honeysuckle cups.

The first cloud that blocked the sun out of my mother's life, Cloud One, came when my mother was ten years of age and her appendix exploded. Bang, her body filled up with poison. She was on holidays with her family in County Kerry at the time, playing mermaids on a cold beach underneath a big purple mountain. When she fell over on to the sand and her body began to fill up with the poisonous poison, her little dog barked and licked her face and called out to her handsome family to quickly get an ambulance, for God's sake!

'Somebody call an ambulance, this kid's in trouble!' yapped Hector. Just like Skippy the Bush Kangaroo, Hector knew how to handle an emergency. The ambulance travelled miles and miles over stony country roads with my child-mother inside it. Past houses huddled into the necks of hills, past oil lamps flickering in low squat windows, past families on their bony knees praying for the repose of their souls with their rosary beads in their muddy fingers, which is what people did in the olden days for entertainment. Because this was all a long long time ago, long before electricity and *The Late Late Show* and night-and-day midi dresses and fishnet tights and beauty spots drawn hard on your chin.

My mother didn't feel the broken road underneath her, she didn't see her father's round, weather-brown face, and even rounder spectacles, peering into her own; she didn't see his tears. She didn't notice him checking and rechecking his fob watch as the miles hobbled by. My mother was somewhere else entirely, halfway to heaven, on a stopover in limbo, playing hide and seek with all the unbaptized motherless babies, waiting in the queue for God's divine love.

When they reached the hospital in Killarney, my mother's small body was punctured by the surgeon's knife and long rubber tubes were put inside her to drain the poison into an enamel basin. And the priest was called up out of his nice warm summer bed, and he stood next to her and anointed her forehead with holy water, because nobody expected her to last the night. But she did last the night, and the next night and the next, and so she had to leave limbo and the pagan babies to their own devices, and return to Earth and pain. Eventually, when she was able, she was moved home to Dublin to lie in her big bed, in the pretty house, to lie still for a whole year until all the poison melted away into a different basin and she could get out of bed and walk again.

On the bus my mother is softly singing the bit in the song where the singer is talking about saying I love you, saying it right out loud. I don't know anyone who does that.

Cloud Two came after my mother had been saved from limbo and was starting to walk again. My mother had spent a year in her high bed in her father's house. A whole year, with a big safety pin laid across the open chasm of her wound, to stop the tubes falling down inside her like snakes falling into a pit. Every few days, during that slow year, Nelly would climb the stairs with long-stemmed lilies, placing them in a tall vase on the dressing table, before tut-tutting at the small ghost between the sheets and going back downstairs to make bread-and-butter pudding and peel more potatoes. The scent of the lilies was very strong, and my little girl-mother didn't like it, but the flowers had been chosen on purpose to disguise the even headier scent of the slowly draining pus and poison that filled the room.

Gradually, though, as my mother's health returned, Nelly spent less time climbing the stairs with cut lilies, and the doctor stopped by a little less frequently, and my mother's handsome older sister, Ellen, rose from her knees, where she had been quietly praying, and started thinking about her own life for a change. Maybe she thought about how close her sallow little sister had come to death, and how thin the line that separated one kingdom from another really is. Like hopscotch squares, smudge the chalk with your toecap and you're out. Maybe Ellen thought about God, and his mercy, and all his angels and saints, and how he and his winged team had brought her little sister back from the dead.

Ellen was a great favourite of the archdeacon, who was a frequent visitor to her father's house. Ellen was a terrific reader; she could recite Shakespeare, pulling her long auburn hair over her mouth and chin to make a beard and talk like a man. The archdeacon liked to call, often and uninvited, to sample Nelly's bread-and-butter pudding and to hear Ellen's stirring recitations (here 'stirring' means making someone's heart beat and ears prick up, not what you do with sugar in your tea).

Green-eyed Ellen, already the recipient of many medals and cups for elocution and dramatic interpretation at the Feis Ceoil (which was a kind of really, really serious talent show, where the judges wore three-piece suits and spoke in Irish), had been asked to join a troupe of actors in a famous theatre in Dublin. The archdeacon liked to talk to strong-minded Ellen about God and mystery, and all the angels and saints, and Ellen, who had just left her convent school with honours in everything, and for whom a career was being discussed, was a respectful and passionate listener.

One day, with a big spoon of Nelly's treacle tart slipping down his throat, the archdeacon had an idea, an awfully good idea, that would protect Ellen from the rough and tumble of theatrical life, where costumes came in baskets and lips were ringed in carmine and archdeacons and their like were consigned to the stalls.

When my mother was well enough, when the lilies had faded and the wound healed, she slipped out of her high bed and walked across the landing and into Ellen's bedroom. Ellen was sitting still on her quilted bed next to her trousseau. No silks or bows, no fripperies or soft promises, no lace, no satin, no netting, no silver slingback sandals, no tiaras. On the bed there were heavy woollen vests, a long white nightdress, a dark heavy blue bathing suit with a great big skirt attached, long black skirts and flat black shoes. The worst of the items on lithe and lovely Ellen's girlhood bed was the swimming costume, weighty as chain mail. As she looked, my mother backed into the bedroom wall. She felt herself slip. And she slipped and she slipped until she hit the bedroom floor, crying a big sea of tears.

Maybe Ellen could have swum in those tears, naked and free, and left the horrible old costume, the skirt embroidered with seaweed and dead mermaid hair and the spittle and phlegm of drunken sailors, to dry up and rot on the shore. Ellen was eighteen when she chose to become a nun; soon she was relieved of her long auburn hair, and she wouldn't get it back again until she married Jesus in heaven.

Maybe in his deepest sleep, the archdeacon dreamt of beautiful young girls with long auburn hair, reciting poetry with pretend moustaches falling over their tender lips. Maybe those kind of girls frightened him.

In the jaunty garage, my mother's handsome brother,

hearing a long wail, lifted his handsome head from beneath the bonnet of his jaunty car. In the long back garden, Madeleine, too, heard the cry, momentarily quitting from drowsily pruning the roses.

Cloud One and Cloud Two, as is the way in stormy conditions, followed in quick succession.

We stand inside Uncle George's Pet Shop, to shelter from the rain. I am careful not to spot the mice.

'It's starting to clear,' says my mother from underneath her red rain hat. There are actual raindrops all over her wet-look coat, her oh-damn-it-I've-paid-for-the-bloody-thing-I-might-as-well-wear-it coat. The hamsters, noticing her startling resemblance to a fireman, are looking around for a fire. The faded parrot is swivelling its head left and right searching for a tell-tale whip of smoke.

'Who called the fire brigade?' whisper the kittens into one another's sharp little ears. Except that kittens speak in French accents, so they actually whisper: 'Oooo called du fyer brigade?'

'We'll risk Arnotts,' she says, stepping out on to the wet street. 'We'll chance the card.'

The communion coat is very smart. It is green and blue, and it has buttons and lining, and at a distance it's a little bit like something you might just see on an air hostess. Forget the sins, things are looking up.

SISTER MARY IMMACULATELY IMMACULATE EVENTUALLY writes down a list of adequate, fit-for-purpose sins on the blackboard, which we copy neatly into our religion copies.

*

'Bless me, Father, for I have sinned. This is my first confession.'

The confessional is shaped like a standing-up coffin.
The door is narrow and hard to open; inside, there is a
smell of fur coats and wet dogs. The priest is behind the
grille. He is locked into his box and I am shut into mine.
We are connected by a wire mesh that looks like the tray
my mother cools cakes on, like the wire tray made of
small squares to let the eggy heat out.

I can't see the priest's face, but his ear is near my mouth,
his head is bowed, like he's already weary of all our silly
childish sins.

'Bless me, Father, for I have sinned. I took the name of
the Lord in vain.'

Not bubbling over with originality, but I'm not lying.
I did it. I really did it. I took the name of the Lord Thy
God in vain. I hurt the Lamb of God Who Takes Away
the Sins of the World with my words and deeds. I sinned
against him properly, so that he had a real sin to cleanse
my soul of, not just a pretend one that he would leave in
the bottom of the wash box.

'Christ on a fucking stick,' my father said that morning
when he picked up the brown envelopes in the post.

'Christ on a fucking stick,' I mumbled in response, enjoying the fresh feeling of the words in my mouth. My
troubles were over. I'd sinned, big time.

'How many times?' asks the darkened priest behind the
cake wire.

He isn't supposed to say that; that didn't happen in our
practice confession. You're just supposed to get three Hail

Marys and a Glory Be and come back in a week.

'How many times did you take the Lord's name in vain?'

'Em . . . seven?' I lie.

'Seven?'

Seven seems like a good number. I'll be seven in a week.

'Are you letting your imagination run away with you?' the voice asks, quite chirpily. 'Are you lying to me now?'

I am lying, absolutely. I am lying, and now I also want to go to the toilet.

'No, I'm not lying,' I lie. My soul will be stained black and blue by the time I get out of this box. Hail Marys are going to be wincing and bruising and sighing and beseeching like there's no tomorrow. Jesus will be scrubbing my soul till eternity. I'm ruined.

'Have you any more sins to confess?' the priest asks, and now he sounds weary again. But Sister Immaculate says we are supposed to say at least two, if not three, sins.

'I stole money from my mother's purse.'

The money sin had been on the blackboard list.

'How much?'

'How much?' I had, in preparation for this very event, taken a half a crown out of her big wrinkled purse and walked around the back garden with it in my fist. Thrice around the dahlias, one wave at the multiplying babies over the garden wall, and I hopped up the kitchen step and put it back in where it belonged. It was our spaghetti money, our beetroot money, our fish-finger money.

'Two shillings and sixpence,' I say, in a haze of misery. Legs crossed against the awful feeling of confinement and needing the toilet so really really badly.

'Three Hail Marys and a Glory Be,' the priest says, and

after absolution I am released from the box. I feel found out, I feel like a really bad person now. A sinner. Weak. And rotten and sinful. Another rotten, weak, bad apple.

OUR COMMUNION IS LOVELY AND VERY VERY HOLY. We receive the body of Jesus from the robed priest, stick out our tongues, squeeze our eyes tight shut and say Amen. Walking back to our pews, we fight him off the roof of our mouths with our tongues, from where he is clinging, doughy and white. But we don't touch him; wild horses would not see us picking at him with our gloved fingers.

We walk in a single white line to the lunch room in our immaculate white shoes, our unscuffed soles tripping from blue tile to black tile to white tile, without a care in the world, Claudette's clickety-clack slingbacks leading the snowy procession. We eat warm bread rolls with butter shaped like little golfballs, and dishes of strawberry jam.

I take my father's hand as we leave the gleaming, highly polished convent, and float all the way to the seafront hotel. Seated at a table within sight of the turquoise swimming pool, he buys lunch for my mother and me, with cash money. Steak and chips and peppermint ice cream, and the who-did-we-not-see-today lady is not anywhere in sight. Nowhere. And I even look sideways for her in the deep end.

After my father drops my mother and me home, and turns the car around, and beep-beeps goodbye, and she kicks off her patent-leather shoes and runs a bath, I look around for my brother. He is sitting at the kitchen table, smoking and gluing the salt and pepper pots to the Formica top. I join him; we've played this game before. There is a new glue on the market that can stick absolutely anything to anything, like stick cars to aeroplanes or something. We regularly test the theory. Quite often we glue the cups to the saucers, and the side plates to the table, and once my brother glued the telephone receiver to its cradle, which sent Anna and Louise into a tailspin because the motorbike boy and the Protestant couldn't get answered, and it made everybody in the whole house shout at him, while I hid under the dining-room table. Once we even tried to glue the heavy black telephone to the Styrofoam ceiling boards. We thought that it would ring and ring, and everybody would be running around in circles looking for it, but nobody would think to look up at the ceiling. But the glue wasn't strong enough, so that didn't work.

He is finished with school, my brother tells me. He is getting a job as a half-share deck boy on one of the trawlers that fish out of the harbour. He will be at sea all week long, he tells me, with the men, and the fish, and the nets and the gutting knives and the heavy smell of diesel. But when the boats come in on a Thursday night, and he with them, and the fish is boxed and weighed on the harbour, and the skipper is paid in a big wad of cash, and when all the crew go over to the Pier Bar and hold on to the bar rail while the pints are being pulled (until they get used to the stillness of the ground again), he'll receive his half-share of the week's takings. Money. Money and freedom. No Brothers. No un-Christian Brothers. He will be laughing, he says, laughing.

Jesus will be pleased, I think, going up the stairs. He's very fond of fishermen.

I go to bed and listen to the radio, tune in to *Late Night Extra* in the newly holy dark. I wait for my father's key in the door. Wait to tell him that I have ten whole pounds to put towards our holiday now, ten actual pounds. I have counted the money that was slipped into my communion bag, in notes and in coins, all through the splendid day. I want to tell my father that we are well on our way to feeling the sun on our backs. I want to tell him that John is going to be a fisherman. That, at fifteen, he's had enough of the Brothers to 'last him a fucking lifetime'. Except I won't say exactly that, because my soul is like a fresh piece of drawing paper, clean and blank and full of promise, and I want to keep it that way.

I want to tell him that I've just realized that the body of Jesus tastes like the back of a stamp. I want to ask him if he thinks about Jesus and Mary and the power of the Holy Spirit, even a little bit. I want to ask him if he thinks Majella will ever get her baby back from the Catholics, if we'll ever go to America, if he and I are going to leave here and live with the snowdrift lady and her golden dog in her low white house by the sea, where I sometimes play alone, or with the dog, on her swivelling high stools next to the barrel-shaped home bar in her living room.

I want to ask him if I will still go to school if we leave here to live with her, and drive around in her low red car, and if I'll see Norah any more, and if it will ever just be him and me any more. I want to ask what will happen to my mother. Will she simply wait in the bath until we leave, or will she reach out for us? I want to ask if Anna and Louise are really my sisters, because I know now that John is really my brother, and I am ready to know.

So many questions in the unanswered-question bin are tumbling over the white sheets, furling up in the tartan blanket; so many questions, so many many questions. But I fall asleep, listening to Peter, Paul and Mary telling anyone who's interested that the answers are blowing in the wind.

Blowing around in the ruddy wind.

6

Naked Apes in Polka Dot

'A N DTUIGEANN TÚ? AN DTUIGEANN TÚ? DO YOU UNDER-
stand?'

'No, Sister Immaculate.'

'*Ní thuigim!* I don't understand! Say it!'

'*Ní thuigim.* I don't understand.'

*Ní thuigim. Ní thuigim. Ní thuigim. Ní thuigim. Ní
thuigim.*

I don't understand anything. Nothing. I'm weak. Stupid.
A dolt. An *amadán*.

Now that I am ten (all of all my fingers), I am weaker
and stupider than ever. That much at least I've gotten
into my thick head. Now letters, as well as numbers,
are tumbling around the page, refusing to join up into
sensible spellings. Plus I have a very sore throat, so it hurts
to speak those hacking Irish syllables.

Sister Immaculately Immaculate is stretched to the pin
of her wimple, what with all the endless note-taking in
her little black book and the waves of litter engulfing the
tennis courts and the patches of three-in-one oil stain-
ing the pathway leading up to the bicycle shed. Not to

mention the infinitesimal speck of dust on St Francis of Assisi's plinth and the hairline crack in St Jude's plaster armour. Poor Sister Disinfect-First-Ask-Questions-Later has decided that we, her class of decade-old mice, are the straw breaking her beleaguered back.

'Gril?' says Sister Do-I-Spy-Waste-Paper-at-the-Bottom-of-the-Tennis-Courts?, holding up my copybook for the entire class to see.

'And what, would you like to tell myself and the class, is a gril when it's at home?'

'Girl, Sister. It's meant to say girl.'

'I see. So we're not being asked to believe that the little boy and the little "gril" were playing cars in the rookery, by which I can only assume you mean rockery?'

Yes, Sister. No, Sister. Three bags full, Sister.

'Life, eh?' says Norah, leaning against the convent wall when we are eventually released from the gut-clench classroom.

Norah has decided that she is going to be a writer. This means that everything that happens to her, good or bad, is 'material'. Material is the stuff that she's going to put in her books.

'What, like material you make a skirt with, or a poncho?'

My mother made me a poncho, out of a tweed skirt she used to wear. She fringed it with woolly white braiding. It's the coolest thing I own.

'Yes, only the material is in your head, not in a shop.'

Norah went to a new hospital, where they tried to teach her to breathe properly, just by talking about things. She loved it there. At night, older girls, made of skin and bones, sat on the end of her bed and told her the stories of their lives.

She left the hospital after a couple of days. She still couldn't breathe. But her material file was bursting at the seams.

My material file has tumbleweed blowing through it. My material file is like a bad Western that nobody wants to watch any more.

Everything stays the same. Life, eh, is like a boulder perched on a clifftop, that's about to roll down and crush the wagon train. Only it doesn't, it just teeters there. Life, eh, can't decide what to do with itself.

Louise and Anna go to work and come home again. They buy beads, and make chokers, and tie-dye their T-shirts. They creep up the stairs late at night, and slam doors in the morning. Sometimes Anna gets a broken heart and then her mascara runs down her face. She and Louise drink tea in their bedroom, with their door tightly closed. They come out again, all cleaned up, when there is a motorbike revving outside the front door, or when Louise's boyfriend (who now also has a beard) pulls up in one of his endless variations of Mini cars.

John comes and goes, but mainly he works on the trawlers that nest on the harbour like big seabirds. He did a navigation course and learned how to read the stars like a route map. The problem with stars is once you start trailing after them, you might never find your way back home.

My mother got a job for a fortnight, playing the part of Maria in *The Sound of Music*. The show was produced by a Musical Society who worked out of a draughty theatre in Drogheda. My father and I went to see her. She was pushed out on stage in a wheelbarrow, stuffed with cushions and covered in something very green, that looked like plastic grass. I think it was supposed to represent the living hills. She sang very nicely and passionately and her lipstick would certainly have been visible, even from the back row.

She stayed in Drogheda for the two weeks, in a bed and breakfast.

'We've a star in the house,' the landlady said over and over, to anyone who'd stop long enough by her privet hedge to listen.

'I was happy there,' said my mother, when she came home. Unpacking her vanity case and kicking her high heels under the bed.

'I was happy there.'

My father and I sometimes visit Snowdrift, though less and less. Her husband is nearly always home when we call now. Polite and friendly, insisting that we come inside, sit up at the barrel-shaped bar, on actual bar stools, and have a drink.

'I Am the Boss!' he reads aloud from my printed T-shirt. 'That's a bit of a responsibility!'

He smells nice. Nice and leathery and rich and warm. He smells like holidays and saunas and important telephone calls. I like him.

'What do you think of this contraption?' he asks me, shaking a silver cocktail shaker.

'It's amazing,' I say.

I don't like to tell him that I've seen it before. That I've played James Bond, Secret Servant, with it, while I was waiting for my father and Snowdrift to finish their meeting in the other room.

We all have a drink. All of us except me and the dog. They only ever have soda water and lime, which neither of us likes.

Norah is breathing steady, leaning against the convent wall and examining a small, grainy, much-creased black-and-white magazine photo, showing some shark-white woman resuscitating a man whose face you can't see (a clipping that her big brother had appropriated from some boy, who was probably, almost definitely, English). To be honest it's pretty difficult to tell what the woman is doing, and I don't know if resuscitating is exactly the right word.

'Life is not for the faint-hearted.'

Things are in turmoil, which is a useful word but not a place you'd particularly want to go on your holidays.

Sister Polish-Anything-That-Moves is on the warpath. She has been made school principal. She is the head nun now, or 'head numb', as my father says, which is not very useful when you're rolling into her classroom at ten to eleven in the morning without having had the stomach to face your Irish spellings, and with your long multiplication so full of rubbing out and starting again that it looks like a small hillock of muddy numbers which some enthusiastic elves have been tramping over in wet wellingtons.

Since her promotion, Sister Immaculately Immaculate

has big pink spots of anxiety burning holes in her cheeks. And her black notebooks, so full of the terribly important, endlessly unsatisfactory things she has to note down, are flapping around her navy-blue habit like a murder of crows.

'Can you have a murder of nuns?' Norah asks, holding the curiously terrifying picture sideways, to get a better view.

'What is that?' she asks, pointing to something on the woman's back that looks like a harness. I lean back against the wall to take a proper look, so full of dread of the bell summoning us back to class that I can hardly even concentrate on the truly alarming photograph.

'I think she's pretending to be a pony.'

Norah looks doubtful.

'Being a decade old is like being ten Hail Marys, one Our Father and a Glory Be old. That's old, isn't it?' I ask Norah in my throat-grated voice, hearing the first shrill hit of the hand-held bell that Claudette, who's now a *prefect*, despite her free will in ballet class, has been entrusted with to round us all up.

'Maybe I could leave school now. Maybe I could just stay at home, or go and draw with my father in an office, or sweep up hair for Anna. Or anything?'

'Being ten,' says Norah, 'is not actually being as old as you think. It's important to remember that you are a human child. It's also important to remember that, if you were a dog, you'd be seventy.'

She refolds the picture, puts it back into her tunic pocket, under her good handkerchief.

I don't want to come into school any more. I wish I

was a seventy-year-old dog, hanging around, doing barking, being weak and stupid, and chasing old cats. I hate school. Haaaate it. Haaaate it. Haaaate it.

I've been missing a lot of school lately. There is a new clock in my parents' bedroom, but it doesn't always have the heart to wake them. Also, I've been sick.

I know that I am sick even before I go into the hospital. I know it as soon as I see the finger-sized men in top hats and tailcoats, walking all over my bed. About a dozen of them, strolling around, waving their canes in the air, going about their shadowy business in the city of my rumpled sheets.

'Do you see the little men with the walking canes?' I ask my brother, who has jumped up on to the garage roof, late one Thursday night, and has tapped on my bedroom window so that I can let him in. He isn't sure if he's forgotten his front-door key or if the key has fallen out from deep in the pocket of his jeans when the men were wrestling him to the deck. He has come ashore with his long wavy hair chopped off.

The trawlers go to sea every Sunday night, motor out from the harbour into the big wide sea, and anchor on the H and H. The H and H is a small square on the grid of the Irish Sea, on a map of fishing grounds. It is a dot of choppy, slapping, deep dark water. For five whole days the trawlermen, the crew, cast their heavy nets and drag for plaice and cod and mackerel, for sole and hake and big grey flat-headed mullets. Mean old fish that look like an argument.

My brother climbs through the window I have opened

for him, clenched by the smell of the catch and in an oilskin jacket blackened by diesel fumes.

He sits down on my bed, among the roving men in top hats. I've been sick for days; the room is littered with used tissues, a MiWadi bottle and jug of water doze on the bedside table, a thermometer sleeps under the bed.

'Do you see the little men with the walking canes?'

'No, I don't see any little men with walking canes. You're hallucinating.'

Hallucinating? So that's what hallucinating is! Hallucinating, when your imagination opens a trapdoor, climbs out of your head and swings down into your actual life. Hallucinating.

My hallucinogenic little men are giddy with pride in their ingenuity, in their invisibility to all but me. But I still don't trust this word. What if you think you are hallucinating, but you aren't? What if the thing has really happened?

My brother is talking. He is telling me that when they got ashore, after five long nights and days on the H and H, and with the fish still gasping on ice in the hold, the men, the crew, held him down on the wet, gut-slippery deck.

'Fucking hippie,' the men said, and one of them took out his gutting knife, while others held him down. And the knife man grabbed up fistfuls of my brother's hair and sliced it clean off. Cast it, shorn, into the sea, for the prawns to nest in.

He is going away for good this time. He has money, wet, hard-earned, fish-scented money, the remains of his half-shares, saved up in the cover of the *White Album*. He is going away, he says, getting the fuck out of here, really, this time, really, really. But I'm not to tell anyone. It is a secret.

I won't. I don't tell secrets.

When he leaves the room and the scent of fishes settles to sleep on my pillow, I think about hallucinating. And I also think about not hallucinating.

Earlier that day, when I woke up, hot and thirsty, from a complicated temperature-led dream about swords and seas and squared copybook pages, she was there, standing by my bed, holding a box of chocolates.

'Contrast,' she said, handing me the box. 'I think you'll like them. They're awfully grown up.' She was alone. Her little dog must have been outside, waiting for her, in her low-slung car.

My mother stood in the doorframe. She looked tired in her faded purple skirt that she made herself on the sewing machine, and her blouse that is a little bit tight now.

'Why are you here?' she said to the pale-golden woman in my bedroom, to the wisp of sunlight standing next to my bed, to the strange, lonely, visible-invisible woman who waits in her house by the sea, with her golden dog and her golden sandals, for my father to call; the woman who is as impossible to grasp, to hold on to, as the mercury in the thermometer under my bed.

Why are you here, I wondered too. Why aren't you at home in your feathery, lovely house with your husband, who purrs nicely like a cat, and who is kind and warm and small and interested?

He doesn't know that we visit his home when he is not there, not just when he is. I don't think he knows. I don't think he knows that we sometimes see the person that we do not see, the person who is standing in my bedroom, looking like she is waiting for something to happen, waiting maybe for the sun to come out from behind a cloud and guide her to the exit.

'Why are you here?' asks my mother. She doesn't sound angry; she sounds tired. So so tired. So so tired.

I HAVE MY TONSILS TAKEN OUT IN AN ACTUAL HOSPITAL. First in the operating theatre, where there are bright lights, then in a recovery room, where there is bright blood, followed by four days on a ward, in a high iron bed, opposite a pale-green girl who gasps for air and looks like a fish that has been left flapping on the quayside.

All this 'turmoil' is followed, however, on the last day of my recuperation, by a takeaway knickerbocker glory from the Italian cafe on O'Connell Street. Louise brings it in for me. Dragging the reluctant Protestant into the ward with one hand, and clutching the welcome ice-cream tub in the other, she is bursting with news.

'I'm kind of engaged,' she says, looking worriedly at the paint-stuck window frame, which doesn't open, which probably hasn't been opened since the olden days when they sawed people's legs off with a kitchen knife and left the nursing to a jar of leeches.

Louise can't concentrate unless she's next to an open window.

'Are you claustrophobic?' I ask her, through a mouthful of strawberry and vanilla ice cream and glorious syrupy peach.

'Don't be silly,' she replies. 'I just can't breathe indoors.'

Her boyfriend settles himself on the end of the bed to read his motoring magazine. He seems entirely indifferent to Louise's fresh-air ailment, which is probably just as well if he is going to be living with her in midwinter. She has a puzzle ring on her finger, which wasn't there the last time I looked. When she takes it off, for me to try on, the pieces of brassy gold unravel like a ribbon.

'Are you sure this is an engagement ring?'

'Yes,' Louise says. 'Make a wish.'

I don't like making wishes. I'm torn between making all the wars in the world stop and a sun holiday in Minorca. ('Ya daan't wanna go to Majorca no more,' Dawn's mother reliably informed me in the ladies' room of The Club, while she dabbed at her mouth with her lipstick, occasionally missing her lips and anointing her teeth. 'It's full aw goddamn tourists. Minorca. Minorca is where you wanna go.')

I'd like to go somewhere full of tourists. I wouldn't care if tourists were end to end in my hammock, playing canasta with their teeth. I'd go anywhere. Somewhere.

I opt for travel and say a quick wishette for world peace. Louise puts the ring back on her finger. Her now fiancé, absorbed in his magazine, also has an important new addition to his person: bright-orange elephant-flared corduroy trousers, flapping over his skinny ankles, which are sticking out over my neatly secured hospital-bed corners.

'Engaged?' I ask, looking from the deafening trousers to the knotty ring.

'Yes, more or less,' she replies. 'We're engaged, right?'

she shoots at Elephant-Flare Boy, who is too wrapped up in an article on the joys of Swarfega to reply.

Louise is twenty now, which is weird. She finally has a job she likes, working as a display artist in Arnotts. She is the person who screws on the models' arms and pulls their tights up over their unbending legs. She creates pictures behind the shopfront glass, to show people what they should look like. To show them how ordered and precise and matching and nicely ironed and uncomplicated things could be if only we all had rods of steel screwing us into the ground and were made of plaster instead of blood and guts and dangerous freewheeling free will and swollen, ulcerated tonsils.

Louise and Mr These-Also-Come-in-Lime-Green! plan to rent a basement flat near the harbour. She's thinking of getting unused plaster knee sockets, and some spare wrists and hands, from the display room, and screwing the disembodied limbs on to the walls of their new flat, and then spraying them with 'instant cobweb' that comes in a tin.

'Why?'

'It'll look interesting,' she replies. 'Different.'

But I don't mean that kind of why. I mean why is she leaving home. At this rate, there'll hardly be any siblings left.

I am discharged the next day. My father picks me up, bringing small gifts for the nurses, wearing aftershave and his best tweed jacket. Everyone smiles and waves as we leave the ward. I look back at the fish girl, the girl without gills, pumping her arms up and down, maybe to salute our departure, maybe to get a breath. I hold my father's hand tighter, understand my extraordinary luck, my unique good fortune. Outside, he is driving a Mini that looks suspiciously like the one Louise's 'fiancé' usually drives.

'Yes,' my father says. 'I borrowed it.'

Soon after my escape from hospital, Louise takes me to visit her almost-mother-in-law. Mrs Fiancé is very nice indeed. She has a long stretched lawn that looks like it has been hoovered, and spotless fitted carpets, and a hostess trolley, and she is wearing a twin-set with a matching string of pearls. And, pretty astoundingly, she makes us home-made Viennese biscuits, which I chew up very carefully before I swallow and which are so perfectly perfect they look like they came from a packet.

I don't see why Louise has to marry her boyfriend in the first place. I think she should just go round to his big airy house for her tea, sunbathe on the lawn, push the hostess trolley over the pristine carpet and sit on the windowsill breathing all the fresh, clean air and eating his mother's Viennese fingers.

Marry! Marry means forever, till death do you part, or at least until you go blind looking at his ruddy trousers.

Sometimes, when Dawn and I play among the sawdust and wooden blocks of the boatyard, where her father's boat is kept for the winter to be scaled and scraped and cleaned and varnished, where we hide ourselves among the oily engine parts and musty rigging, building castles for her Sindy dolls under ripped tarpaulins, sometimes, in the shadow of the big wooden stilts that hold the boats aloft, we discuss the kind of boy she plans to marry.

Dawn changes her mind a lot. She doesn't think

anyone will want to marry her, because she is taller and broader than all the boys we know. She says she doesn't really mind who she marries anyway, not that much, not as long as she can have a colour television and plenty of nougat and take her favourite doll, Bettina (who cries real tears), with her. The best bit of marrying, as far as Dawn is concerned, is that she'll never ever have to eat rolled-up tongue again.

Unfortunately for Dawn and her guests (usually me), rolled-up tongue is her mother's signature dish.

'Tuuuungue,' she calls, like a Wild West rancher, and we hide.

I don't want to marry anyone, I tell Dawn, especially not someone with orange corduroy trousers. I would prefer a dog. And a black dog, with brown eyes, would be the icing on the cake.

'What cake?' says Dawn. 'You won't have a cake unless you get married.'

I don't tell Dawn that marriage is not for the faint-hearted, that marriage means lots of cloud-staring and angry rows that crash about our kitchen late at night like big rolling seas. Marriage, I have begun to realize, can seriously interfere with life.

Marriage was the biggest cloud on my mother's horizon, the one that got in the way the most. It was nice at first, she says, when they had a gracious flat in Dublin town overlooking a pretty square, when they had friends around to admire their rooftop view, when they motored to Connemara in a burping car and tumbled on the rough, wet sand. And when they ran through Dublin in the rain to the pretty old theatre, whose doors genuflected out on to the street, and bought seats in the gods, and sat together in the redolent dark, eyes shining.

But marriage meant babies, and babies begot more babies. They were all my father's babies after all; it's just that he didn't really notice them, because as soon as they were in his world, he moved to another world, a world he hankered after, yearned after. While my mother steeped their nappies in a big pink bucket, my father looked for his cravat and his car keys and clicked the door shut behind him.

'Then you were born,' my mother sighs, her eyes flat, a chipped china cup in her shaking hand. '"Oh," he said, "look, a baby, a little baby!" "Yes," I replied, "another one."'

But that was later, that was much much later. That was just before the end.

It is the weekend. I am declared officially better. Norah has come round to inspect the open goal where my tonsils used to be, and now she and my mother are shelling eggs, to make sandwiches for Louise's engagement party. My mother is pushing the hair off her face, and not really bothering too much with her lipstick, and she's leaning against the kitchen counter and forgetting what she's supposed to be doing, and every few minutes she looks out the window like she's expecting a message from the clouds.

My father is out, I don't know where. He borrowed the fiancé's Mini and left.

'I'll be back,' he said, 'when I can.'

He's been coming and going at all sorts of strange

hours, even turning up once or twice at dinner time, startling the returning husbands on our road, with their newspapers and empty flasks and panting Cortinas. Many of them have never seen him before.

He has come through the door at the end of the working day, walking around the corner from the bus as if it is the most normal thing in the world, making my mother and I look up in surprise. We ask him to reach for a beetroot bottle, while we look for cream crackers. We take money out of the big red purse, run up to the shops and buy a tin of picnic salmon, wonder if he'll still be there on our return.

If he stays in, it is for an hour or two. He paces up and down the kitchen, walks into the living room, straightens pictures, leans against the back door to have a cigarette, big swollen sighs blown out of his insides with the escaping smoke. He borrows a couple of quid from my mother, who stands staring at him, and kicking the washing machine with the back of her heels, before she gives it to him; he winks at me and leaves. We get back to normal.

He can't telephone to say he's running pretty ruddy late any more; the telephone has been cut off. It just sits, silent as an angry cat. Black and warm and curled up on itself on the hall table, not speaking to anyone.

It's not entirely clear why we're having a party for Louise, who seems vaguely uninterested in the whole idea. No one is terribly sure if this is an actual engagement or a flash in the pan. If it wasn't for Norah suggesting that we get on with the egg sandwiches, the whole notion might have taken off like a startled crow.

It was Anna's idea to have a party for Louise in the first place, and Anna's at work. Saturday is her busiest day. She'll come home tired, and with swollen ankles, and wait for my mother to get out of the bath so that she can have one herself.

Louise spends most of her time in Protestant land, for which you can hardly blame her, and Anna has rarely been back home before bedtime either. Not since the big row, when all Anna's clothes were thrown out the bedroom window and landed outside on the front grass. Her clothes got ejected because her side of the girls' bedroom was so so messy. Airborne, Anna's clothes made an interesting flock. The neighbours came to watch them, the bellbottoms and minis and maxis and midis, feed and peck at the front lawn. They watched the garments lift their buckles and belts skyward to see which way the wind was blowing, in case they decided to fly away all together. To take off.

I don't know who threw Anna's clothes out, or why now, all of a sudden. Anna's messiness, just like Louise's open window-ness, is simply who she is.

Louise and her fancy-fiancé will definitely come to the party; it's their night. And all of their friends, the boys with startled beards and leather jackets, and the thin cold girls with poker-straight hair and lots of eyeliner, will come too. It will be like a regular Saturday night in our house, except this time featuring egg sandwiches.

But nothing feels normal at the moment. Even normally abnormal things feel abnormally abnormal.

Before all the strange strangeness, before the car disappeared and my mother started forgetting to put on her lipstick, before my father stopped discreetly pocketing the bills and final demands, and before he started just throwing them on to the growing heap on the kitchen table, before all that, when the phone was still miaowing and my brother was here to have important meetings underneath the dining-room table, and before Louise was engaged, and before Anna's clothes ended up in the garden, Saturday nights were predictable.

On Saturday nights, my parents used to go out to The Club and I got babysat. Being babysat meant that someone, usually Anna, gave me money to go to bed. Sometimes, if she and her friends really wanted me out of the way, one of the bearded leathery boys would carry the television up to my room on his shoulders, and endlessly adjust the bunny's ears until I could see *Hawaii Five-O* in pristine black and white. I didn't mind being babysat; I'd lie awake and listen to the music, the Beatles, the Rolling Stones, or, when Louise was home with Corduroy-Boy, lots of cow-bells and folk music and ladies from England singing about country fairs and cheese.

Sometimes, when the music was shaking the walls and making my teddy dive under the bed with his paws over his ears, I'd get up and sit on the top of the stairs in my nightdress, and breathe in the lovely woody smoke, which floated up the stairs from their untipped cigarettes.

Then, just before my parents would return, as if by magic or some secret signal, the leather-jacketed boys and platform-soled girls would get on the bikes and disappear down the road, the neighbourhood foxgloves, peeping up at the departing hordes from over a garden wall, shaking their trumpeting heads in their wake.

Anna was often among the departing tribe on the back of the bikes, racing away down the street, leaving a pillow shoved under her candlewick bedspread pretending to be the sleeping her.

It was another kind of secret, one that you kept tight for fear of actual death by her icy stare if you ever, ever, breathed a word of her secret departures.

My mother and Norah are planning on making lots of egg mayonnaise sandwiches, with the crusts cut off. I'm supposed to sit at the kitchen table and butter the bread with butter that has been left in the sun to soften. That is my job, mainly because eggs, like milk, make me want to throw up.

My mother boils six eggs for the first lot of sandwiches, puts them in the egg bowl and then forgets what she is meant to be doing and goes to have a bath. By the time she has stewed, wrinkled, dried and de-wrinkled again, she's forgotten which of the eggs in the bowl are hard-boiled, and which raw.

She and Norah, in an attempt to separate the cooked from the uncooked eggs, take *all* the eggs from the bowl and spin them across the countertop like figure skaters. The hard-boiled eggs gird their loins, hang on to their tutus and spin, magically adhering to the shiny surface. The uncooked eggs, however, who only ever wanted to be lightly scrambled or to take their place in a Madeira sponge, say their hurried prayers and go skittling off the countertop, landing, smashed up and yolk-bled, on the floor, further casualties of our kitchen war.

Norah and my mother think that egg-spinning is a

hysterically funny way to spend the afternoon. Me, I don't agree, not one little bit. I don't trust all the gaiety that the broken eggs are unleashing.

I leave them to their egg games, go upstairs to look out of John's bedroom window, stand on his stripped bed, see if, by any chance, he might be on our road, heading home for the party. He isn't.

My mother has been acting increasingly strangely, getting stuck, stony and unblinking, in front of the mirror, like Lot's salty wife. Either that or she has been so busy painting walls and darning the bald bits on the stair carpet, and washing out the cupboards and lining them with sticky-backed plastic paper, that her fingers soar and multiply. She made me a nightdress and a dressing gown for me to bring to hospital, from remnants that we found in Hickey's fabric shop. Only there weren't quite enough remnants for the nightie, so she made the straps out of a check napkin and then cut flower petals from the rest of the bits of the napkin and sewed them on to the nightdress to make it match, so it didn't look like I was wearing a napkin in the first place.

Other times she sits, stock still, on the kitchen step, staring at the washing line. She has started smoking again, blowing smoke out of her cigarette, fast and mouthy. Not like my father, who drinks in the smoke so deeply you would forget it was ever there.

Sometimes my mother is frightened, and frightening. One night before I had my tonsils out, when I couldn't sleep because my throat was sore, and *Late Night Extra* on the radio was over, and even the shipping news was over, and even the radio was over, heading off to bed to put its rollers in and prepare for another day of broadcasting, I went down to the kitchen. I wanted to see if my father had, unknown to me, come home and gone straight into the kitchen without saying goodnight, because he thought I was asleep.

I opened the kitchen door quietly, stood under the fluorescent light watching her smash pots and pans around while she figured out a way of keeping his dinner hot. Usually she'd set a covered plate of food over a pot of gently simmering water, keep an eye on it during the ad breaks on the television, so that when he came home his food was hot. But that night he was so late the water had burnt off.

She turned and saw me, pale and white under the bleached light, and she opened her mouth and screamed and screamed and screamed. She thought I was a ghost, she said, a child ghost, slipped quietly out of limbo, come to take her back. Later, she sat at the kitchen table, drinking brandy from a teacup, brandy left over from last year's Christmas pudding.

'When you were born,' she sighed, eyes flat, the chipped china cup in her hand, 'he said, "Look, a baby, a little baby!" "Yes," I replied, "another one."'

She was staring at me, to make sure I was really a human. 'I'm not a hallucination,' I told her. She nodded. I thought to myself that this would be quite a good opportunity to confront her about Santa Claus, about whom I had my suspicions.

'He's not real, is he? Nobody can look after every single body, can they? Nobody can mind everybody.'

'No,' she replied. 'They can't. He's just a story.'

THREE IMPORTANT FACTS, NOW THAT I'M A DECADE OLD and have no tonsils.

Fact one: although Protestants do, for the most part, have hostess trolleys and cupboards full of gooseberry jam, they do not have black marks seeping out from their souls and creeping up to bruise their necks. We all have the same souls, greyish fish, under our ribcages, not unlike the 'insoles' grown-ups slip inside their shoes.

My new friend on our road is a Protestant. She is beautiful and has golden skin and pleated skirts and brown eyes and also a long-haired dog. We play hop-scotch on the pavement outside her house, and lie on her bed under her Donny Osmond posters, listening to 'Puppy Love' with our eyes closed. If I was God, I'd be ruddy miserable if she wasn't at my table. If I was God, I wouldn't give a damn who was a Catholic and who was a Protestant, and I'd divide up all the money in the world equally, so that black babies wouldn't be starving and having to have their pictures stuck on the side of collection boxes, and I wouldn't allow people to send final demands, and I'd make the big black bin bag full of returned cheques with the word 'dishonoured' printed on them, the big black bag sitting in the bottom of my parents' wardrobe, disappear.

Fact two: money rules the world. Not God or kings or presidents or even the Pope.

All the hissing and spitting around the kitchen table could be quietened with money. All the roaring bills struck dumb by money. All the promises of getting the hell out of this place, and seeing some of the world, fulfilled by money.

Before, when we always had a car, he and I would drive along the winding back roads to the airport. We'd park the car and go right inside, like golden people. We'd go upstairs to the half-moon bar, order our drinks and then, glasses in hand, we'd stroll outside on to the viewing balcony and, sipping our Coca-Cola and our breath-metal whiskey, we'd watch the planes take off into the big open sky.

'One day, Billy. Some day.'

Or we'd drive out of the estate, in winter, past low dark fields and lonely horses, to the boatyard. We'd watch the boats being lifted out of the water, brought to the yard and propped up on gigantic wooden stilts, and washed and tended and nursed.

Here, the crew would scrape a boat's weed from her bow and belly and hull. They'd varnish and paint her, and smoke and shout and climb up and down ladders to the cockpit to take the engine apart, and mutter and curse, until it was time to go to the pub. Dawn and I, bored of our games in the sawdust, tired of inventing lovers and husbands, liked the boatyard pub; there was a permanent set of Christmas lights strung around the mirror behind the bar there, and heavy wooden stools, and a poker-hot fire always alight in the small grate.

Money. Bloody. Ruddy. Money.

Eventually, as round after round of black pints and golden whiskeys filled the small wooden tables, Dawn and I would get bored in the ancient boatyard pub. We knew that we'd never get home in time to have our tea, or dinner, or supper, or whatever anyone called it, we knew we'd be too late to watch Bruce Forsyth giving away toasters and electric blankets and hairdryers and fluffy toys on *The Generation Game*, so we would ask our fathers for money. Then we could walk to the shop at the crossroads, in the blue-black dark, to buy sweets.

The last time we were there, in the boatyard pub, I knew. I knew, and I didn't want to ask. I hated asking. I could see the sword swinging plain as day.

'Ask!' said Dawn. 'Ask!'

And I did. I asked.

He took some coins out of his pockets, not enough, gave them to me, looked at me, and without speaking, asked me not to ask for more. I didn't. I will never ask again.

Fact three: although some people find great amusement in egg rolling and party planning, things on the whole are a bit empty. A bit scary. Soon there will be no one left.

John is in Amsterdam. He sent a postcard of a canal, with very little writing on it. He didn't say when he was coming back. Louise and Fiancé-Man have had to change tack about living in a basement flat with cobwebbed body parts on the walls, because his parents don't really approve of their way-out notions. Louise is going to live in a proper house, with an upstairs and a downstairs and electricity bills and an unexciting boiler. And probably Anna; they've never really been apart.

Louise looks confused by how quickly her interesting and far-out ideas for living have dried up.

Norah goes home before the engagement party starts. Her chest is sore from laughing, tight from the scent of the eggs. She leaves before the boys with beards and leather waistcoats arrive on their motorbikes and drink cans of Guinness and talk about horsepower and rubber dinghies. She leaves before Louise's friend Maria practises her ballet moves on the kitchen table. She leaves long before my mother gets out of the bath and takes the sandwiches out of the fridge. She leaves long long before my father comes home, looking like he has lost something. Someone gives my father a drink, and he sits at the kitchen table and looks up at the Styrofoam ceiling, where there are still stains from all the breakfasts that have bounced off it, and stains too from John's and my aborted attempt to glue the now-useless telephone to it.

He looks up and says: 'I should have been a painter. Why wasn't I a fucking artist?' And he calls my mother's name, and asks her, 'Why? Why wasn't I a fucking artist?' And there are tears and rage gathering under his face, and he can't see me because I am invisible behind the noise and the dancing and the lousy guitar playing, and the inhaling and the exhaling and the dancing dancing dancing. My mother looks at him for a long time, and then she says she doesn't know. 'Why is anything the way it is?' she asks.

And then the ballet girl starts singing the Judy Collins song, and Anna comes in from the garage, having spent quite a long time out there with a leather jacket around her shoulders, sitting on its owner's knee and blowing smoke rings at the ceiling, and when she hears my mother join in the sad, bleating song about the clouds that get in

161

the way and those ruddy ice-cream castles, she goes right
back out there again and lights another fag.

MY MOTHER, DESPITE HER SUCCESS AS MARIA IN A WHEEL-
barrow, is cheesed off with her future as a singer. The
band Four in a Bar (a name which makes my father
wince, and then wince again) is not exactly *Top of the
Pops* material.

'The band isn't really going anywhere,' she says, her
back to the kitchen table, her front facing the electric
ring, stirring mushrooms and fried bread around in the
pan.

'Except to homes for the bewildered,' mutters my father.

'Anyway,' continues my mother, 'the bass guitarist is
having thoughts about the priesthood.'

'Joining?'

'Leaving.'

'How rock'n'roll.'

Her back stiffens.

My mother isn't sure what to do next. Once, when I
was smaller, she got a summer season singing in Butlin's,
which is a kind of carnival, a holiday park, with a crowded
indoor swimming pool and an empty outdoor swimming
pool and crazy-golf courses and talent shows, where some
families spend their summer holidays.

'Can *we* go to Butlin's?' I once asked my father.

He didn't grace my question with a reply.

I went to Butlin's with my mother once or twice, on the
train, when she was employed there, got in on her staff
pass. We took sandwiches. I sat in a chair-o-plane to eat

mine, in the rain and the mist, while she went backstage and changed into her singing dress. But the people on their holidays didn't really want to be entertained by a soprano, especially one singing about moody clouds, which only served to remind them that they hadn't had as much as a glance of sunshine all week.

The audience really only liked when the comedian sang about his extra leg, diddle-iddle-iddle-um, and anyway the money was lousy and the night was long and the journey back to our suburb on the smoky train cold and miserable, and my mother said she'd rather eat Lucky, the very depressed budgie, than go back there, cap in hand.

So that's that decided: she's going to be an Avon Lady instead of a singer. Ding dong.

'Four in a Bar have had their day,' she tells my father, who is at the table, eating his brunch of mushroom and fried bread, and massaging his temples behind his newspaper.

Brunch is a useful word. It means that you're so unbelievably late for breakfast it's pretty much lunchtime. Nobody else on our road eats brunch; I've checked.

'Did you hear me? I said Four in a Bar were finished.'

'I suppose Three in a Bar could, if the participants were willing, be vaguely more alluring,' says my father, and is rewarded, a short time later, with electrocution.

I don't think my mother meant to put the earth in the live, and the live in the earth, when she was changing the plug. Whenever things around our house break down or fall apart, my father says 'get a man'. He usually says this when he's on his way out the front door, glancing at his watch and running the tip of his tongue over his dry upper lip. When the door clicks shut behind him, my mother repeats 'get a man, get a man', and then does the ruddy job herself.

It's probably just as well that my father is the one she instructed to plug in the kettle, after her spot of rewiring, because, as everyone later said, a smaller man would have been blown clean through the Styrofoam ceiling. As it is, there is nothing but some jagged scorch marks around the socket, and after a couple of days his heart stops missing beats and settles back to normal.

On a scale of one to ten, in terms of glamorous and attractive jobs, with continuity announcers being an undisputed ten, air hostesses being a solid nine, and hotel receptionists and travel agents weighing in as at least a seven and a half, if not an eight, Avon ladies, despite their zippered cases, their free samples and their willing smiles, are probably about a two.

When my mother was a singer, with flowers pinned to her tiny waist, she once saw Maureen O'Hara backstage in the theatre that my mother was performing in, flanked by her two big handsome brothers, one at either elbow.

Maureen O'Hara was so tiny she looked like she had been carved from a wisp of willow. She was, my mother said, a natural beauty.

Maureen O'Hara had won a beauty contest run by a soap manufacturer, and the first prize was a screen test in Hollywood. All the girls who had entered alongside Miss O'Hara knew from the moment they saw her that they didn't stand a chance.

We are repacking my mother's Avon case, which I had

unpacked in awe and wonder the night before. We are preparing for her first foray into the outside world as a saleswoman.

'The secret of retaining natural beauty, any old bit of beauty at all,' she says, looking around the kitchen for her sample soap-on-a-rope, 'is to keep your face perfectly still. That's what Maureen O'Hara did, all those years, waiting for her screen test: she kept her face perfectly still. Like alabaster. Still as death, so as not to promote lines and wrinkles. Where is the damn soap?' she asks, her face creased with irritation. 'It's their biggest ruddy seller.'

I walk up the stairs, with my face set in stone, to retrieve the soap-on-a-rope from under my pillow. I am not going to move a single facial muscle until I get a screen test.

Avon ladies go door to door, selling cosmetics from their little turquoise cases, and only get paid if they sell something. But the contents of the case are truly magical.

There are face creams and hand creams and body lotions and bath balms; there are lipsticks and rouges and foundations and palettes of baby-blue eye shadow. But nothing comes near the incomparable, the most irresistible of all the treasures in my mother's neat little case: Soap-on-a-Rope.

Self-explanatory and utterly far out. I covet it.

My mother's job is to walk up and down our road, knocking on doors and convincing our neighbours that with just a kiss from the eye shadow duo, and a sprinkling of dusting powder, they too can look like Gina Lollobrigida.

First, though, before she can begin her sales patter – 'Let me show you what a clever hint of highlighter can achieve' – my mother has to get her foot in the front door.

She has to battle through the neighbours' resistance, ignore their suspicious peeps through the venetian blinds, greet with sunny optimism the cautious scrape of the front-door chain, take it on her powdered chin when their shadows retreat behind the frosted glass. Once inside – if she's invited inside, that is – she has to negotiate the holy water fonts dotted around the door frame, traverse the transparent rubber matting covering the good hall carpets and sit at our neighbours' Formica-topped kitchen tables, under the glare of their fluorescent bulbs and the stern, interested-despite-herself gaze of the Virgin Mary from her perch over the kitchen sink.

Most of the ladies on our road are very welcoming when she calls, offering cups of tea, examining her scented produce with giddy interest.

'Where would I be going with a firming day cream, when it's at home?' they laugh, offering my mother a Rich Tea biscuit and another drop of 'hot'.

I like to stay close to her heels, slip into their kitchens in her shadow. I'm eager to display the Soap-on-a-Rope, to stand still in my kneesocks, my face in frozen pre-screen-test mode, doing a fine job of imitating a bathroom hook, the soap swinging from my crooked finger.

'No,' says the woman in the next house along. 'No. No no no no no, out, get out! And you can close that garden gate on your way.'

The morning after the egg party, there is no one in the kitchen except Louise and Anna. They are sitting at the table among the memories of the night before, the window wide open behind them.

I have engagement cake for breakfast. I'm eating the iced 'io' in congratulations.

Anna is going to be Louise's bridesmaid. They are both going to be wearing the same dresses, long and ruffled, with big polka dots on them. Louise's dots are black and Anna's dots are red. They say that the dots are their sins. Louise and Motor-Man are going to get married in a Protestant church, because it has daffodils in the garden and there won't be too many long prayers, which is handy because Louise doesn't believe in God, she believes in a book called *The Naked Ape*.

'What's a naked ape?' I ask her, swallowing a petal that someone, somewhere, had so carefully iced.

'All of us,' she says. 'We are all naked apes. Naked hopeless apes. Apes in polka dot.'

The living-room table is scattered with empty plates. At least the sandwiches were a big success.

7

Kneesocked Soldiers of Christ

'THERE IS A LIGHT AT THE END OF THE TUNNEL,' Norah whispers, when I creep to my desk on Monday morning, a morning rapidly skidding towards noon. 'There's a light at the end of the tunnel, and it isn't the train.'

Sister Mary Immaculate has had to hire another teacher for us, a teacher with a red polka-dot dress and legs in tights, and a hairband, and glasses and a lovely wide smile. Her name is Mrs Barrett, and she is English. She is the first non-numb teacher we have had. She will be our teacher for this, our confirmation year. I am overwhelmed with gratitude. Flooded with relief.

I almost say a quick prayer of thanks to the Virgin Mary, but I stop myself. I'm getting sick and tired of the Virgin Mary, mooning around, gazing up at the weather, while stupid, miserable things happen that she could so easily stop. Holy Mary, Mother of the Divine Jaysus (as my father likes to call her from time to time), kicking back her heels, up there, among the angels and saints, on her viewing platform in the sky. She could have just waved her magic wand, or rattled off a quick novena, and the gutting knife that sliced John's hair off would have slipped from the trawlerman's grasp and disappeared into the oily sea.

She could have made the men in shimmering suits, with the ice melting in their heavy glasses in that thickly carpeted hotel bar, finally buy my father's cartoon drawings for America.

She could have made the nuns allow Louise and Anna to stay in school, instead of sinking back into her fluffy white cloud, searching for her rosary beads among the raindrops while my sisters knelt on the classroom floor, with chewing gum stuck to their foreheads, waiting to be told to stand up so that they could be expelled properly. She could have minded them a bit, looked after them, instead of making them go to work every day.

While we're at it, Virgin Mary, Hail Mary, Mary Queen of Peace, any chance you could roll up your plaster sleeves right now, this minute, and start sorting a couple of things out? Could you maybe stop my mother sitting on the back step, staring at the empty sky, and then dragging herself upstairs, as if she's walking through sand, to lie in a lukewarm bath for so long her skin looks ready to peel away? Might you see fit to glue up our postbox and stop all the hissing post from landing on the mat? Or maybe you could strike down the postman with something chronic and instant like a bolt of lightning?

Do the words 'Remember, O most gracious Virgin Mary, that never was it known that anyone who fled to thy protection, implored thy help or sought thy intercession was left unaided' ring any bells?

My earth mother collects the post every morning now, Mary, wringing her hands at the bottom of the stairs, waiting for the metallic gape of the letter box. Netting the manilla catch before my father has a chance to chuck the whole lot into the kitchen grate and throw a match in after them.

The explosive post, once opened and read, makes the doors slam and the cutlery smash around in the drawers, and the house steam and burn. The letters open up trap-doors in my parents' throats. Words once left unspoken are released to fly around the kitchen, mean little sprites refusing to retreat, to be trapped back inside the speaker's weary body.

Old Damocles is having a field day.

Oh, I don't know, Mary. Mary, Mary, Quite Contrary. Maybe you're a little bit scared of such an enthusiastic adversary. Maybe you don't have the strength to rip his sword from his fist and hurl it into eternity.

Let's face it, there's plenty that you pretend not to see, Mary, plenty you'd rather not get drawn into, for fear of getting your hands dirty. And maybe that's just the Virgin Mary way it goes. Maybe God has you under his big planet-squash thumb, Mary. Maybe your alabaster hands are tied.

My mother cannot swallow. This is quite a recent development. But she doesn't know a song about that.

'I can't swallow,' she says. 'I. Can't. Swallow.' And she waves her hands in front of her throat and rushes, gagging, to the sink. 'I've a bone in my throat,' she gasps.

She drinks Pure Lemon Juice by the neck, from the

bottle in the fridge, and the bone temporarily dislodges itself. She allows herself to swallow Slimcea biscuits and grapefruit segments and lightly toasted fat-free Nimble bread.

Then she rushes all the way upstairs to lie singing in the pink bath. She can swallow in the bath.

When she's not gagging, dieting or recovering in the bath, she's running up and down the seafront, wearing plastic pants over her trousers; paddy pants, the kind that babies wear over cloth nappies. She thinks that dashing around in plastic pants, and lashing into the PLJ, and having slimming biscuits and skinny bread for dinner, will make her thin and wispy and blonde and willowy.

It won't. She gets hungry after a few days, and cracks.

Cracking means walking up the road to the whistling grocer, with the endlessly surprising lisp and the biro behind his hairy ear, and buying a fresh batch loaf. She eats at the kitchen table, butter and jam on the knife, while the radio plays songs that make her sigh or, in some cases, dart up out of the chair to turn the damn thing off.

Sometimes during the cracking and uncracking game, my mother goes on the 'chicken and white wine diet'. This is her absolute favourite, but sometimes she cracks on that one too, and has potatoes with her chicken, and a second glass of wine, and maybe a splash of gravy and just a little bit of ice cream.

'Christ,' she says to her reflection in the long wardrobe glass, 'what are you doing? What are you doing, you stupid bloody woman?'

I don't know who she sees in the mirror, but it is a different person from the one I see. She says she's enormous.

A fully grown male kangaroo is enormous. Cathedrals are enormous. Apollo 11 is enormous, was enormous. She's just a woman who fits a narrow bath. But what do I know?

MRS BARRETT, THE LIGHT AT THE END OF OUR TEACHER tunnel, being English, doesn't speak Irish.

Every day, after big break, Sister Germicidal comes back into the classroom, for thirty agonizing minutes, to teach us how to say stuff in the Irish language that we just might need at some unimaginable stage in our lives.

'*Téann* Daidí agus Mamaí agus Pól agus Íde cois farraige sa ghluaisteán.'

'*Chuaigh* Daidí agus Mamaí agus Pól agus Íde cois farraige sa ghluaisteán.'

'*Rachaidh* Daidí agus Mamaí agus Pól agus Íde cois farraige sa ghluaisteán.'

There was an awful lot of coming and going to the seaside in the family car. Maybe they should have brought a tent.

'Maybe tomorrow Daidí agus Mamaí agus Pól agus Íde will drive over a manky cliff,' Norah whispers, between breaths, while I try to look invisible and count the minutes until Mrs Barrett's gentle knock on the classroom door.

Joy and astonishment. Astonishing astonishment. We are going to Australia with Mrs Barrett! The entire class. Australia! We drew our passports yesterday, and today, after little break, we are boarding the aircraft and strapping ourselves into our seats. The flight will take about twenty minutes, and will include in-flight announcements from Claudette, who may also be doing a little bit of free-will dancing in the aisle while she's checking that our seatbelts are properly fastened.

When we land, we will be applying sun cream and cork hats, and going exploring. We're looking for wombats, kangaroos, ostriches, koala bears and Aborigines.

Norah suggests that we all get vaccinations before we go. Claudette isn't allowed to be the nurse, because she is already the air hostess, so Norah gives out the injections herself. She has quite a lot of experience of injections, because she spends lots of time in hospital while doctors and nurses try to find out why she can't breathe. In the end, Norah isn't allowed to use her compass for the vaccinations. Mrs Barrett says she'll just have to use her imagination instead. 'It's certainly sharp enough,' she tells Norah.

We'll need to drink plenty of water in Australia, because of the soaring temperatures, and also we need not to accidentally stand on a funnel-web spider. In the event of emergencies, Claudette is packing her nurse's uniform and a plastic stethoscope in her school bag.

Mrs Barrett says that our Australian trip is a 'project'. I didn't even know the word existed. This is our 'Australia Project', and when we are finished we are going to do another project. The next project will be called 'My Autobiography'. An autobiography is a book about yourself, a whole, entire book. Somebody better alert Sister Immaculate.

'Never start a sentence with I,' Sister Clean-as-a-Whistle says. 'I don't want to see any Is at the start of your sentences.'

Sister Immaculate must think that starting sentences with I is a grubby, selfish thing to do.

I don't care what she thinks.

I am happy.

I wake up early in the morning.

I run to school.

I can't wait for their alarm clock to ring. The apologetic little alarm that I can hear from their bedroom across the hall.

I walk to school with my friends from the road, who go to the national school. We walk together as far as the old Protestant church, before we turn our separate ways. While we walk, we make plans for the afternoon, usually hopscotch and a bit of lying on someone's bedroom floor listening to their Gilbert O'Sullivan single. The nuns still don't allow us to speak to the national girls when we're in our private-school uniform. I think that that is the most stupid rule in a school full of stupid rules.

I say goodbye to my friends and run down the convent drive, hang up my gabardine, skip to my desk. I'm there, waiting, when Mrs Barrett opens the classroom door and says: 'Good morning, girls! Are we ready for our day?'

Sister Immaculate, if her burning cheeks are anything to go by, feels duty-bound to remind Mrs Barrett, and the class, ever so nicely, of course, that, albeit we have an entire continent to explore (my, aren't we the lucky girls?), we also have a CONFIRMATION to make.

Confirmation is a sacrament, whatever that is, and is

about as dull as the name suggests. We are to become soldiers of Christ, by means of an awful lot of praying and, interestingly, choosing a saint to name ourselves after.

On our confirmation day we will go to the church, sit upright and prayerful in our pews, and, when we are called, troop up to the bishop, who will be waiting for us underneath his mitre, his crozier at the ready. We'll promise to serve God with every fibre of our being and, while we're at it, promise to be teetotallers. He'll give us our saints' names, and some extra blessings, possibly with the aid of something unctuous (although I may have got that wrong), and, hey presto, we'll be confirmed. Simple as that.

Teetotal means never letting a drop of alcohol pass your lips. This promise is also known as 'taking the pledge'. Once the pledge is taken (which only happens in your mind, there is no actual pledge to hold), you are honour-bound to drink tea for the rest of your life. Tea, MiWadi and an occasional ginger ale, but never alcohol. Alcohol interferes with your free will. It makes you weep and shout and scratch, and sing with tears and mascara streaming down your face. It makes you miss an easy ball on a snooker table, and forget to phone to say you'll be late home. Very, very late home.

Unlike First Holy Communion, confirmation is not at all cheery. Like curly kale, or fried liver, confirmation is bitter and strong and necessary.

We mice can't be confirmed in the convent chapel, because it is too small. It's too girlish and pretty to make soldiers of us. We will join all the other children of the parish in the big echoing church that sits slap-bang in the centre of our village.

We will wait on the long bleached wooden pews, looking left and right, at the depressing pictures of Jesus being whipped and beaten and spat at on his way to his crucifixion. And when we leave, having received the bishop's seal of approval, we will be fortified, renewed in Christ. We will have a brand-new hardheaded God to sling over our shoulders. Like a rifle, this hard-hearted, grown-up God will protect us, mainly from temptation.

I abhor (one of Norah's most useful words) the ugly big church where we are to be confirmed. I've been sneaking out of the house and going to early Mass there on Sunday mornings. I've decided to give it one last shot, before I hang up my rosary beads. I worry that if I just stop believing, and it's all actually true, that Mary will be bruised black and blue, and that Jesus will have to endure thorns being pounded into his skull for eternity. That's a lot of responsibility. That's a lot of pain to inflict, just because of doubt.

I've been getting out of my bedroom window as soon as I hear the crows wake, out on to the garage roof, gripping the guttering with my hands and knees, dropping down on to the garden wall, stepping over the flowerbed and out the gate, to walk to first Mass with my friend from up the road, the boy who I play cars with in his rockery.

He and I are on a mission.

There is a confirmation story in our religion book about a girl and a boy called Sarah and Simon (that book was definitely written in England). In the story, Sarah and Simon go to early Mass, every Sunday without

176

fail, even though their lazy non-pledge-making good-for-nothing-parents don't stir from their tangled beds. Rain, hail and snow, Sarah and Simon struggle to Sunday Mass, becoming such devout soldiers of Christ that eventually their slovenly parents are shamed into getting up, finding their Sunday shoes and skipping along to Mass beside their children. And the family have a perfect life from then on, perfect and prayerful and ordered and calm. Nothing left to worry about at all, except running out of shoe polish and not being able to find your mantilla.

I hate the big church: the radiators rattle and the priest speaks into a microphone, which makes him sound like he's in a swimming pool. Babies wail, mothers pinch, fathers hiss at fidgeting children and sneak despairing looks at their wristwatches. I can't bear looking at Christ's agony looming out of the walls. I look at balding heads that flake and freckle. I look at the women's scarves, catch the scent of their hairspray, wonder how long more till breakfast, how long before I can allow myself to abort this mission.

'Do you like Mass?' I ask my friend on the way home, trailing down our drizzling road.

'God, no,' he replies. 'I just like a bit of fresh air in the morning. My brother is an awful farter, and I'm in the bottom bunk.'

'Do you believe in God?' I ask him when we arrive at his gate. His Manx cat is staring at us out of the box-bedroom window. The net curtain falls behind her. She looks like she's on a stage, miaowing, silent and indignant behind the glass.

'Of course I do. Everyone believes in God. Are you sure that's an actual question?'

*

When I get home, my father opens the front door. He has been in the kitchen, looking for the Alka-Seltzer. His mouth feels like a desert. He has found an orange, squeezed the juice, poured it into a glass. He sits on the stairs to drink it. I tell him about my mission.

'Smoke and mirrors,' my father sighs when I mention to him all the people Sister Immaculate knows about who went to Lourdes and ended up hopping out of their wheelchairs and dancing a jig, because of the sheer power of the Holy Spirit.

'Jiggery-pokery, Billy. Smoke and mirrors. Smoke and ruddy mirrors. For Christ's sake, stay in bed next Sunday and read a damn book.'

THE SAVING GRACE ABOUT CONFIRMATION IS CHOOSING your saint's name, which will be written on a certificate and signed by the bishop, and which will be part of you. Forever.

Claudette wants to choose Donny. Saint Donny.

'There is no Saint Donny, Claudette, and no Saint Osmond either,' says Sister Immaculate, her eyes closing in despair. 'Have you considered Mary?'

Claudette is going to whisper 'Donny' all the way up to the altar, and all the way back down again. 'Donny. Donny Donny Donny Donny Donny.'

I want to choose Elizabeth, but Sister Immaculate says she's up to her teeth in Elizabeths and I can be Paula instead.

'Paula?' asks my mother. 'Christ.'

On Thursday our class will fly home from Australia, so that we can concentrate on God for the night, and on Friday we will be confirmed. My father will meet my mother and me, afterwards, in town, he has promised.

We land on Thursday afternoon, jetlagged, just before the bell goes.

Mrs Barrett looks around the class when the aircraft has ground to a halt, before we disembark, while we are all still strapped into our seats.

'I'll be thinking of you tomorrow,' she says. 'And sending you my very best thoughts and wishes. Have a wonderful day, and remember: we all have our crosses to bear.'

She looks around the class.

'Each and every one of us has our crosses to bear.'

I hear Norah's rattle-breath spike gently in my ear.

'Some of our crosses,' says Mrs Barrett, 'are not easy to see.'

On Friday morning I button up my navy-blue Crimplene dress with the smocking and the leg-o-mutton sleeves. I pull up my white kneesocks and put on my pancake hat with the navy-blue bow. Sister Immaculate picked out the hat and sent our mothers into Arnotts to buy it. We special privileged mice will troop down the aisle of the big hungry church in our specially purchased pancake hats. We will stand out from the crowd, we battle-ready, kneesocked soldiers of Christ.

I am looking at my reflection in the oven door, waiting by the empty grate, my hat at a jaunty confirmation angle. I am waiting for my mother to apply her finishing touches, so that we can walk down to the church together, when the radio goes off.

It dies, right in the middle of the weatherman telling us to expect rain.

'Rain is exp—'

Silence. The fluorescent bulbs crackle and die. My mother comes into the kitchen, mascara wand in hand, checks the light switch: up, down, down, up, nothing. She turns on the electric cooker rings: nothing. Plugs in the kettle: it is mute. She goes into the hall to phone the man from the electricity company, to ask him to come and fix the lights, to ask him why we've been plunged into silence, and remembers that the phone is still cut off.

I look at the final-final demands rolling around the kitchen table, clutching their sides in mirth. Whispering 'I told you so', and sniggering up their envelopes.

The electricity has been cut off. We will have to find candles, and an old saucepan to boil water over the kitchen fire. There's no time to sort these things out now. We close the door behind us on the silent house.

I wonder if Mrs Barrett's husband works for the Electricity Supply Board. Maybe she knew. Maybe she was talking just to me. Maybe the darkened kitchen is a cross to bear.

We walk up the road, my mother in her tweed cape and her leather gloves, her patent-leather high heels, her red lipstick colouring her mouth.

After the bishop has dispensed with us, and we have trooped out of the church again, Claudette's ringlets snarling around her Donny-less face, my mother and I cross the road and wait at the bus stop.

We wave brightly at my classmates revving by, some in Jaguars, others in coughing Cortinas, and take the bus into town.

We are to meet my father for lunch in the thickly carpeted hotel, the hotel where he and I ran that day to escape the mad rain and the thunderbolts and Damocles' itchy sword. The hotel of the suited businessmen and the snowdrift woman who turned down his dampened collar with her icicle fingers.

My mother stands in the foyer, looking around for him. She is worried by the opulent carpet, by the whispering, reverential receptionist, by the honey-coloured, flock-paper walls. She is unsettled, skating between her glittering smile and the uncertainty in her eyes.

'He'll be in the bar,' I say. 'It's this way.'

I haven't seen the snowdrift woman since the day I awoke to find them both standing in my bedroom, my mother by my bedroom door and, melting slowly next to my bed, with the chocolate box in her pale-blue hand, Snowdrift.

Something was won that day, or lost.

My father waits for us in the bar. He is smoking un-tipped cigarettes from the yellow box, fast, like he is rushing to catch a train.

'Gotta give these damn things up,' he says, by way of greeting.

'Druids get you, Billy?' he asks. 'Are you too holy to eat?'

'I didn't take the pledge,' I inform him. 'I used my free will.'

'Good decision. I'll drink to that.'

'Electricity's been cut off,' says my mother, tapping one of his cigarettes out of the box. 'We're going to need candles.'

I watch him write a cheque for lunch. He found his chequebook, and other chequebooks found him, followed his scent. It will be at least a couple of days before this cheque hits the bank. And who knows what might happen in a couple of days. Something perfect might happen. Something extraordinary. The something we've all been waiting for. The one big event that will turn the lights back on.

Maybe all those early Masses will spur the Blessed Virgin into action; maybe she will intercede, have a quick word with God. Or maybe someone here on earth will do something, someone here in this whispering restaurant, where suited men mingle with nylon-stockinged women, kicking their big ideas over the tufty carpet. Here, where glasses clink and laughter bubbles, and waiters bend like dancers, and potatoes steam under delicate herbs, and my mother reapplies her lipstick, checking her reflection in the soup spoon, leaning back in her chair, closing her eyes. My father stubs out his cigarette, lifts his glass and, before swallowing his wine, says: 'Cheers, Billy, don't let the druids get you down.'

'Cheers,' I say, raising my Club lemon with ice.

'Cheers,' says my mother from the rim of her gin and slimline tonic.

The waiter brings me salmon. It's not from a tin. Things are definitely – I can feel it, there's something in the air – things are definitely looking up.

8

My Autobiography

PRIVATE-SCHOOL SUMMER HOLIDAYS, THREE MONTHS instead of two, stretch long and pale in national-school suburbs. Norah is in hospital, again. Dawn is in Minorca, again. I play hopscotch with myself on the empty morning road, bounce two tennis balls off the garage door, reciting bouncing rhymes.

'A, my name is Annette, my husband's name is Arnold, we come from America, and we sell apples. B, my name is Billy, my husband's name is Boris, we come from Barbados and we sell boils . . .'

I wander up and down the road, past net-curtained windows, carefully observed by pink-eyed poodles and inquisitive indoor cats. Inside, back-combed mothers dab nail varnish on laddered tights, get on with making loaves of spotted dick and soaking grimy shirt collars in basins of Daz. I meander past, remembering their almost iden-tical kitchens from my mother's and my brief careers as Avon ladies, recalling their Formica-topped tables, their top-loader washing machines with the sinister wringers that could flatten your fingers to a pancake, their stoops

and gardens. On their kitchen walls hang framed procla-
mations and burning sacred hearts and portraits of John
F. Kennedy, dead and debonair, glowing underneath his
polished glass.

There is a saying, embroidered on to a velvet cushion,
on Mrs Mac's fireside chair: *Níl aon tinteán mar do thinteán
féin* ('There is no fireside like your own fireside'). You can
say that again, Mrs Mac, as long as you've got your teeth
in.

We weren't very good Avon ladies. We gave away the
samples and failed to sell much more than a decorative pot
of talcum powder. Our customers, it seemed, were happy
to stick with soap and water, with Pond's cold cream and
a dab of all-purpose lanolin, with a lick of Atrixo for their
detergent-raw hands. A proper Avon lady in an irritated
Volkswagen drove all the way out to our house to collect
the turquoise-zippered case.

'That's bloody that then,' said my mother to her reflection in the sunburst mirror in the hall, the clatter of the
Avon lady's slingbacks still echoing down our path. Somehow we forgot to return the soap-on-a-rope to the zippered
case. It hangs in the endlessly occupied bathroom, worn
down now to a fish-shaped sliver and a ropy memory of
scent.

Up and down the road with two tennis balls and a piece
of chalk, looking at other people's houses. Looking over
garden walls, at unblinking windows and unyielding front
doors. Venetian blind, venetian blind, net curtains, venetian blind, net curtain, gnome.

Gnome. Gnomes in Mrs Ryan's garden. I pause, lean on

the wall, watch the little men cast their fishing lines into a decorative mirror.

Mrs Next-Door-to-Gnome comes out, to deadhead her chrysanthemums and wash her windows with vinegar and water. She's a busy woman.

'Aren't you the lucky girl, all of June ahead of you?'

'Yes,' I reply. Meaning no.

She doesn't look like she thinks it's lucky not to be in school for the whole month of June. She looks like my loitering presence is utter nonsense. Nonsense, nonsense, nonsense.

'There's a fucking gnome on the road,' my father announces. 'A gnome!'

We are getting ready to go for a spin in the new car. When I say new, it *was* new once. It's a low white car that makes quite a lot of noise when it takes off, and the boot doesn't actually open, and it's not great in the rain, because it leaks a bit and my father, who is tall, has to fold up his knees and bend down to get into the driver's seat. But it goes. It goes, and the steering wheel is gripped by leather, and the wipers work, and the neighbourhood fathers, alighting from their consistent Cortinas, nearly drop their empty flasks in astonishment when they first see him sputtering down the road in it like a badly wounded James Bond.

I'm not sure exactly what my father's job is now. I watch him stand in front of the hall mirror, from my perch on the stairs; I watch from my lair, on the balding stair carpet, behind the wrought-iron railing, watch him fold a crisp handkerchief into the breast pocket of his sports jacket, comb his hair over his head. He puts his pencil case and his drawing book and his sheets of Letraset into the slim leather briefcase he carries, checks again to see that he has packed a scalpel to sharpen his pencils.

He says goodbye to me, tells me he'll be back before I go to sleep. I hear him tackle the ignition, and when it revs up, surprising even itself, he drives off up the road, the exhaust raging and snorting like a taunted bull.

He rarely comes back when it is still light. When he does, he stands around, unsure of what to do next, as if he doesn't quite recognize his surroundings in the glow of evening. Massaging his five o'clock shadow, eyes darting towards the kitchen clock, he usually just collects his sailing gear and leaves again, pausing on the porch to check the wind direction.

We are getting ready to go out. It is Saturday. He is wearing a soft tomato-red shirt; he is edgy, checking and rechecking his reflection in the sunburst mirror.

'A gnome!' he calls to the closed kitchen door. 'A gnome!' he calls up the vacant stairs. 'Christ on a fucking stick. What is wrong with people?'

Nobody answers.

I like the gnome. Gnomes. Now there are five gnomes in Mrs Ryan's garden.

'The gnomes are multiplying,' he calls out to my mother's tight-shut bedroom door. 'Someone needs to spay the fucking gnomes.'

We drive out along the coast road past the seafront hotel, swing right, cross over the isthmus and enter an enchanted land of pretty houses running down to the sea and enthusiastic over-bred Labradors running after our banjaxed motor. We drive past her house. Past where she used to live. We haven't been there for a long time. Months and months. Three children are playing in her garden. A dark-haired woman takes plastic bags of groceries from the back of a station wagon, calls to the children to lend a hand.

He slows down. We watch the tiny movie of these other lives. One of the children turns to watch us watching them. Solemn brown eyes. She's holding a yellow melon. We drive on.

We drive up the green hill, past high walls and closed, confidential gates. We wind our way up and up, on narrow roads that look like they have migrated from a fairy tale. A twist, a canopy of trees; we turn again. To our right, the bay below is glittering and sun-scattered; to our left, there are two stone pillars with great big carved birds perched on top. Sentinels. We turn into the driveway. We cross our fingers and will the stuttering car up the sweeping gravelled incline to the stately front door. We stop outside. It's just as well. The car couldn't have gone any further than the mile or two up the road it travelled from their old house. It couldn't have taken another breath. It's panting, it needs a drink of water, it needs a bloody Anadin.

Her nice small husband, with the tan and spectacles and soft jumpers, who always hunkers down to smile and say hello, opens the front door. He walks out on to the gravel to greet us. He is carrying a glass of bluey ice. He is wearing slip-on shoes, or maybe they are slippers made of leather.

My father gets out of the car, unfolding himself like a picnic table. We go inside. The house is like a reception room for heaven. It is white and glassy and silver, and strewn with sheepskin rugs and low-down furniture. There are still no children's drinks. I sip a tonic, sitting carefully on the edge of a creamy, leathery chair. She is in another room. I know she is in another room, even though I can't see her. Her invisible presence hangs in this room like a piano note. Already played, over, but lingering.

Her little dog runs out to bark at us. In truth, her little dog doesn't look particularly pleased to see us. He skids to a halt, suddenly, mid-woof, on the polished floor next to my chair. The little dog forgets his lines, stares at me for a moment, starts licking himself.

The two men talk about boats and conditions and offshore winds and the Fastnet Rock. The damn rock, eh? Some fucking rock, that is. There are photographs on the wide mantelpiece, of the nice man looking busy and smart at the shoulder of some shrewd, suited men who look like the men that are nearly always on the six o'clock news. The house is so high and so soft we could be sitting on a cloud. I wonder if we all might float away. They finish their drinks. I leave mine on a side-table. I don't like it. We stand, we leave; we pump the accelerator, hold our breath. He watches from the step, unsmiling, waves from the generous front door when the spark catches. We drive away, watched by someone trapped behind the glass.

MRS BARRETT RETURNED OUR CORRECTED AUTO-biographies on the last day of term. Mine is under the dining-room table. Mrs Barrett's verdict, written in red biro on the last page, reads: 'Very much better this term, I am delighted!' She even included the exclamation mark, to show that she was really, truly happy.

It's not that good an effort really. There are loads of bad spellings in it, and rushed drawings, and it's definitely not even half as good as Norah's autobiography. Not even quarter as good. Norah sellotaped the baby teeth she'd been saving on to the pages of her project, and cut off a bit of her hair with pinking shears, and stuck that in, too, alongside her ten inky fingerprints.

Norah's autobiography is a loud, brilliant shout. Mine is more of a stutter.

Bored with the lonely road, I sit under the table to re-read it. Some of my autobiography isn't the truth. One chapter in particular, called 'What I Think Is Wonderful', is, as Norah says, 'almost entirely fictitious'. We had to choose three wonderful, awe-inspiring, things to include. My three wonderful things were: 1 My father; 2 God; 3 Computers.

I felt obliged to mention God, because everyone else did and Norah said that I would be a total idiot not to mention computers, which are big machines in basements that can do maths and time-travel at the press of a button. '1 My father' was the only true thing on the page.

Some chapters are neither true nor untrue, they're somewhere in between. I wrote that I had blue eyes that are deep and fathomless, because Mrs Barrett was concentrating on expanding our vocabularies. 'Deep and fathomless' is just embarrassing. I wrote that I want to be a painter when I'm old, and live in Switzerland with a big black brown-eyed dog, which kind of is true and also is kind of impossible to imagine.

I wrote in my project that I had a mother and a father and two sisters and a brother and a four-bedroomed house under a red roof, with a front and a back garden, and a gate that swung open, and a postbox for the postman, and a porch for the caravan lady where Norah and I like to sit and talk, and that is true. Mainly true. But true doesn't stay true forever. True changes its shoes and applies its finishing touches. You can be true one day, and hope to stay that way forever, but then the wind changes direction and blows you east instead of west, and before you know it you are untrue.

At three o'clock I go back out and wait at the top of the road for my friends to reappear from national school, to turn the corner in their pleated tartan skirts, to slope down the road, their beige kneesocks wrinkling around their calves, satchels full of homework weighing down their shoulders. I sit on their garden walls while they finish their multiplication and Irish spellings, their hurriedly learned history of dolmens and torcs. I wait while they wash down their haslet sandwiches with beakers of milk, and get permission to come out and play. I wait for us all to become one.

THE ELECTRICITY IS BACK, BUT THE PHONE HAS BEEN dead for so long now we should really consider burying it in the back garden along with unlucky Lucky, RIP.

Lucky was lying on the floor of his cage one morning, when I came down to pour out my Rice Krispies. Solid and still, and his beady eyes wide open. He'd been right as rain the day before.

('How could you tell?' asked Anna. 'He just looked totally cheesed off, like every other day.')

Maybe Lucky died from boredom, maybe he died from his dreadful life. Maybe he got sick of looking at the same old Polyester curtains beyond his cage, fluttering in the endless breeze from Louise's open windows. Maybe he got sick of the table full of unpaid bills. Maybe he'd had it up to his feathered neck with breathing in other people's cigarette smoke, and listening to the lousy weather forecast, and the bells of the Angelus ringing out from the radio every day like a long slow siren, a long slow call to death.

Maybe he got sick of the midnight threats. 'If she shows her face here again, I'm going to slit my fucking wrists.'

Maybe Lucky was perch-weary, maybe he died of decorative-swing fatigue. Maybe he'd had it up to ruddy here with dandelion leaves and Judy Collins renditions and his misty little cage mirror reflecting his own indignant beak, his own unchanging markings.

John and I put Lucky in a cornflake box and bury him underneath an explosion of dahlias in the flowerbed at the bottom of the garden. We lie back on the scratchy grass and try to think of something nice to say about him.

'He was a bird of exemplary dullness,' says John, in a slow, undulating imitation of a priest's sermon. 'A budgerigar as dim, futile, profitless and stale as a long drizzling Wednesday in the month of March, with nothing more entertaining on the misty horizon to capture your soul than the hole in your stigmata-stained sock.'

'He was,' I murmur in reverent response, 'a wart on our ruddy palm.'

'Amen.'

We lie still under the moody sunshine, the grass on our backs, the threat of squally rain eavesdropping on our conversation, and John tells me about his trip, from which he has recently – palely, silently – returned.

In Amsterdam, he woke up in a room of shattered windows. He looked around at marble-white faces framed by matted hair. At skeletal bodies and bruised limbs. He describes walls decorated with delicate arcs of blood that had spurted from fragile veins. Empty needles littered a floor caked with dried vomit. He sat up, found his friend and groped his way out, towards the light. They were charmed, himself and his friend. Circumstances prevailed. Someone from his friend's family was sent to find them, brought them home. Brought John back before things slipped beyond his grasp, before he ended up in a cornflake box with the marbling bird.

He is never going to hang around for long after Louise's wedding. He is always going to go away again. Maybe he will find work, crewing on a sailing boat that will nose out beyond the harbour wall and head out to sea. A boat that might pick up a strong wind, blowing abeam of Finisterre, that will pick up the Portuguese trade winds, swing west, follow the Gulf Stream, meet a piping wind from the Azores, and blow whatever little boat he is sailing on all the way to South America, maybe even to Africa.

My father talks about the sea in exactly the same way as John, but never *to* John. My father speaks about running with winds and riding squalls. My father is a brilliant sailor. He has been chosen to crew on famous racing boats with the best sailors in the country. He is happiest in these moments, I think. Proud and calm and purposeful, with no broken telephones or hissing post or melting ice women or boiling wives or long neat suburban roads or quietly anxious little girls to knock the adventure out of him.

ON THE NIGHT BEFORE LOUISE'S WEDDING, SHE AND Anna drink Kiskadee and Coke at the kitchen table. They paint each other's nails and take the plastic sheaths off the polka-dot wedding dresses that have been hanging up in their wardrobe, among their belts and buckles and flares, for weeks.

'Fuck,' says Louise. 'It's real.'

'Fuck,' says Anna. 'I know it is.'

Louise gets married in a pretty Protestant church with spring flowers blossoming under an ancient tree. The ceremony is short and friendly. There is no scourging or whipping or blood or thorns in evidence on the simple walls, just quite a lot of appliquéd wall hangings from the ladies' sewing circles, depicting bountiful spring and hope eternal. My nun-aunt, my mother's sister, is not allowed to leave her convent to attend the nuptials, in case she is infected with something un-Catholic and turned into a twinset-wearing, Viennese-finger-making, tweedy-skirted

Protestant. Which, on the evidence of Louise's entirely pleasant wedding ceremony, may not be the worst fate in a volatile universe.

My mother polishes her patent-leather shoes with Vaseline and puts on a short black dress with red and green piping on the sleeves and skirt. My father shaves in the bathroom mirror and unpacks a mauve shirt from a plastic wrapper, which he wears under his only proper suit, which is grey and a little bit dusty. My brother wears a beard, and a borrowed pinstripe suit, miles too big for him, an acquisition made that morning from a willing friend.

'You look like a surprisingly unsuccessful pimp,' my father says, passing him on the stairs.

'You're looking pretty shit-hot yourself,' my brother replies.

My mother's guitar-playing friends, from her now defunct band, pick her and me up in their square red car and drive us to the church. They had made Louise her wedding cake, and decorated it with a little racing track made out of icing, with a matchstick mini-car speeding around on a marzipan track, complete with a little bride waving a starter flag.

My father drives Louise and Anna to the church in a green Volkswagen that is so old it looks like it needs a nap. The car materialized from somewhere shortly after the low white car died, quite decisively, in the night. There was no waking her the following morning; no amount of prodding her with the ignition key, or pressing her accelerator for favours, made the slightest impression. She drew her last breath in our quiet suburb, after a life of shooting around dappled lanes and burning rubber on tar-black highways.

They take so long to arrive at the church there is talk of maybe retiring for a cup of tea and coming back later. I think that the Volkswagen has broken down. Anyone who has seen the Volkswagen fears, assumes, that it has broken down or maybe has had a sudden belt of arthritis en route or maybe needs to go home to put its teeth in or change into its slippers.

It wasn't the car at all. They stopped off in the pub on the way to the church, nipped into the old boatyard pub, pulled up a couple of barstools under the unseasonable fairy lights and ordered three whiskeys.

'There's time to change your mind,' my father said.

'I'm fine,' said Louise, 'but hey, thanks for the thought.'

Afterwards we go to a hotel for our dinner, during which my father stands up to make a speech.

'Good of you all to come,' he says to the assembly, my aunt and uncle, the groom's nicely turned-out family, Louise and Anna's bearded, eyelinered friends.

'I'll be in the bar,' he says, 'accepting drinks,' and then he sits down again.

Louise and her husband (*husband*, Christ-on-a-stick, as my father says) are going to the Isle of Man for their honeymoon. Anna is going with them, to keep Louise company while the groom watches motor racing, and also because Louise and Anna have never really been apart. I'm definitely not invited on the honeymoon. The Isle of Man is hardly Minorca, but at least you could honestly say you'd been out of the country.

'They roll witches down hills in barrels of spikes on the Isle of Man,' I tell Louise as we are leaving her wedding reception that night, my mother, my father and I, to hobble home in the Volkswagen.

'I'll be careful,' Louise says, and then she is gone.

There are so many types of silence. The ones I least like are when you're stuck in the back of a tiptoeing ancient car.

'I'll be in the bar accepting drinks!' my mother finally repeats. 'Is that a speech? Did I miss something? Was I temporarily deafened by a chicken drumstick? I'll be in the bar accepting drinks! Christ almighty, no one's going to forget that in a hurry.'

'WE'RE GOING TO KERRY.'

My mother is ironing her bellbottoms. Her red vanity case is open on the kitchen table. She has already packed the spongy rollers that she can sleep in, alongside her false eyelashes and her cold cream.

'Kit sent a postcard. She's expecting us.'

My mother and I visit her Aunt Kit, in Kerry, every summer. We take the train to Killarney, where Kit's gentle, reliable husband picks us up in his gentle, reliable car and drives us along narrow roads to the other side of the big purple mountain overlooking Dingle Bay.

Tomorrow we will chug out of Dublin town on the Killarney train. We will leave behind the empty morning road. We'll leave behind my father, to oilskins and back bars and boat decks and the foyers of elegant hotels.

My grand-aunt has a whitewashed holiday cottage

perched on the edge of a bay, with blue hydrangea around the front door and a terrifying, nightmare-inducing outdoor toilet out the back that you have to perch on the edge of to go to the loo, not allowing yourself for one second to think about toppling backwards into the chemical pit beneath. Indoors there are wildflowers in a jug on the kitchen table, and an open hearth, and there are roses growing around the window frames. The cottage is like an imagined cottage, like a cottage you would draw with crayons on a clean white page.

By day we drink tea on the beach from a flask, usually with our anoraks on. My mother swipes the drizzle from her back-comb and scowls at the clouds, and sometimes, in a burst of sunshine, we paddle in the pale-green water. Between showers we walk with Kit and her husband up the leafy, winding road to Sheila's post office. Kit's husband buys me a windmill on a stick, and I buy a stamp and a postcard of a donkey to send home to my father.

On the walk back, we might run into the children from the neighbouring farm. Their farmhouse looks bleak and cold. It looks like a solitary tooth growing up in the middle of a bare, windswept field. I don't know how to play with the farm children. I don't know how to begin. The girls have long black hair and long pale legs. The boys have serious faces, and sticks to drive the cattle up the shaley road. I stand under a dripping tree with my plastic windmill, wait for them to pass. I'm like a fairy with no Christmas tree. I look like I'm waiting to grant them a wish. There is nothing that they want from me. They glance, and keep on walking, scaling the long hilly road ahead.

When we get back to the cottage I write my postcard to my father while Kit makes the tea. My mother blows smoke out the window, the vapour from her cigarette running into the mist like water into ink.

'Wish you were here,' I write. What else is there to say?

On the last night, with our bags packed, Kit and I battle long and hard over gin rummy and test our memories in Pelmanism, blindly pairing cards spread face down on the scrubbed table. My mother joins us at the end for a couple of games of beggar-my-neighbour, the exhalations from her mild cigarette sweet and soothing.

I leave the adults, go to bed in the little back bedroom where my mother and I sleep, the bedroom with the ill-fitting door and the friendly smell of banished must, the bedroom tucked in behind the kitchen. My mother's cold cream and cotton wool, her spongy night-time hair rollers, are on the bedside table next to her narrow bed.

I turn on Kit's transistor, settle down to sleep. I still don't sleep without the radio on. Even on holidays. Especially on holidays, where there are no stairs for my father to climb, no night-time conversation to be had with him, no reassurance of his presence, no evidence that he hasn't vanished into his other world.

I am almost asleep when the radio begins to play my father's favourite song, 'What a Wonderful World'.

'Louis Armstrong died today in his sleep, in his home in Queens,' the disc jockey says over the opening bars of the song.

'Satchmo is dead,' he says. 'The world has lost some of her beauty.'

The radio opens up its throat, and the notes and lyrics pour into the little bedroom, flooding it like moonlight.

The disc jockey sounds so sad. 'The world has lost something precious,' he says. 'Things will never be quite the same again.'

I want to tell the adults that Louis Armstrong is dead, and that they are playing my father's song on the radio.

I sit up. My foot hits the floor. I am about to get out of bed when I hear, clear and unbroken, my mother's voice. She is talking and talking and talking, her voice breaking with anger. She is telling her card-shark aunt and tea-towel-folding uncle the great big, cloudy, rain-soaked, thunderous story of her marriage.

Her marriage: the blackest of her clouds, the fog that most efficiently obscures her horizon.

Her words roll for a long long time, like rain over the purple and black mountain that looms up above this little house. Her words drown out Satchmo's velvet tunes. Her words pour. Someone, probably her uncle, makes more tea, heating the pot from the whistling kettle, settling the cups and saucers on a tray.

Her words flood and torrent; her words are a deluge.

'Never mind tea,' Kit says. 'See if there's a bottle of something under the sink.'

My mother's words are boundless. They flow longer than the song playing on the radio, and the next song, and the next song, and the next.

I've heard enough. I sleep.

We go home on the train, my mother and I. We sit in our compartment, with the sliding-glass door and the high brown banquettes, like normal people. We sit, a blonde mother in white slacks, clutching a pretty red bag that matches her mouth, and her daughter, hands neatly folded in the lap of her blue gingham dress, a dress exquisitely made from remnants, carefully bordered at the cuff. We look like a mother and daughter returning from a pleasant visit to the countryside.

My gentle great-uncle buys me a magazine to read on the train. He must think that I am that little girl in the gingham dress, on the inside as well as on the outside. He must think I'm still bloody six years of age; the stories in the magazine are all about dollies in a ruddy dolly hospital having their limbs reset, and dog-eared bears having their stuffing sewn back inside after it has been knocked clean out of them.

My great-uncle hugs my mother on the platform. His soft, tanned country face looks like it needs to go somewhere to lie down, to recover its gentle disposition from underneath the airless story of his niece's inclement life.

There are your own memories, and there are her memories. There are your stories, and there are her stories. There is your imagination, crouching in the luggage rack above your head, afraid to crawl back into your mind for fear that it will run away with itself. And sitting up there, next to your rough and cowardly thoughts, is her red vanity case. Inside her case, there is her cotton wool and cleanser, her foundation and powderpuff, her rollers, her toothpaste, her eyelashes and bright red lipstick. And jostling for a place among these familiar accoutrements, these necessities, these tools for the preservation of face, are all the invisible potions that travel with her: her broken hopes, her dashed expectations, her regret, her fury, her disappointment.

And even without your frightened imagination inside you, you can hear the broken hopes, and hope's bruised friends, pushing and shoving against the flimsy walls of the small red holdall. You can hear all that sadness and rage tinker with the feeble clasp, you can tell that the contents won't be contained for long.

There are a mother and a daughter, in Crimplene slacks and a gingham dress, sitting quietly in the compartment of a train, looking out the window at the green countryside passing by. At a cow, at a sheep, at a pony, at another cow.

Maybe we sleep, as the rhythmic, meditative train makes its steady progress towards Dublin town. Maybe we wake again. Cow-sheep-pony-cow.

Maybe the train's narcotic, sedative progress, the landscape unravelling, green on green, pulls us back to our dreams.

Cow-sheep-pony-cow, cow-sheep-pony-cow, cow-sheep-pony-cow. The train repeats and repeats its mantra, mile after mile after mile. And half-heard, half-remembered, already half-known images from my mother's conversation the night before rise up to the surface. Cow-sheep-pony-cow, cow-sheep-pony-cow. My mother's voice clear and melodic, laying her memories out on Kit's clean table:

'She was always there, always there, always there.

'Always somewhere, somewhere, somewhere.

'He'd say it was over, was over, was over.

'It wasn't. It wasn't. It wasn't.

'When the baby was born – so many years after the

others, so many, many years, who'd have thought it? – he came into the nursing home, stayed ten minutes. Left. He'd hired a nurse; I suppose he felt it was enough. Nurse left, hours before she was supposed to, said the baby is in her basket, and left. The baby was in her basket. I slept. For hours; hours and hours.

'Of course, who knows anything, really? Who actually knows what was going on? Who can prove anything? Who needs to? She was in a clinic down the road. His mistress. They were straightening her teeth. Her teeth. God almighty.'

My mother told her aunt and uncle a long sun-filled story, a story that becomes my dream. They were on a pretty sailing boat in Gozo. A holiday, a rare event, a much-anticipated, astonishingly worldly event. The snowdrift woman and her husband had hired the yacht. Other friends were with them, a lissom, privileged, jaded, suntanned coterie, old hands at cruising around the Med.

My mother, bored with the ennui, tired of sailing talk and dangling limbs, and looks held hot and long over cold beers, went ashore. She stumbled into the local market. She walked among stalls of fruits and vegetables, and herbs and lace, and the traders called out to her in Portuguese because she was brown as a berry and her hair was black as night and her mouth was the colour of the shaded tomatoes, deep red under their canopy.

'I'm sorry,' she kept saying to the traders. 'I don't understand you. I wish I could, I wish I could. I wish I understood.'

They gave her a bag of cherries. Purple.

When she went back to the boat, negotiating with the punt man to bring her back out to the mooring, my father, grim, was packing to leave. He had just had news, on the ship-to-shore radio, that his father, the yellowing Protestant in the high hospital bed, had died.

'I'll come with you,' my mother said. 'You loved him.'

'Yes,' he replied. 'I suppose I did.'

'No,' he continued. 'Stay. Feel the sun.' And he left.

He flew home alone, and my mother stayed on the boat. When he had gone, she poured the cherries into a bowl, offered one to her hostess, the snowdrift woman with the awfully straight teeth, who was lying wilting in the hot shade.

'He has beautiful feet,' the snowdrift woman said to my mother, waving away the bowl of fruit. 'He has the feet of Jesus.'

'Mad,' said my mother to her elderly, rapt relatives in that lovely hydrangea-framed house under the mountain. 'Mad, mad, mad, mad. And he was as mad as she was. What in the name of God were we doing there? Who did he think he was? Christ. He so desperately wanted to be someone else. I knew then. Looking at her, fading away, petulant, furious that he had left. I knew everything, could see everything. "The feet of Jesus." Christ almighty. The feet of sodding Jesus!'

The train has stopped at a station; we are more than halfway home. Beyond the glass the landscape is flat, the sheep have their shit-stained backs to us. The cows don't seem to venture this far east. The sliding-glass door of our compartment opens; a young American woman with plaits and a rucksack asks if we would mind if she took a seat on the banquette next to my mother.

'Not at all,' we reply, hospitable little elves that we are.

'Were you on vacation?' the American asks the polite little girl in gingham.

'Oh no,' the child replies. 'We were on our holidays.'

WHEN WE ARRIVE HOME, ANNA IS AT THE FRONT DOOR. She is smiling. Her back is to the glass panelling. Anna shouldn't be here at this time; she should be at work. Anna shouldn't be smiling so brightly; Anna doesn't do cheery. She's smiling like she's had her cheeks sewn on to her ears.

'What?' says my mother, putting her case down on the porch step. 'What? What is it?'

The bubbled glass around the latch has been smashed. There is a fist-sized aperture, the jagged hole since covered up by a folded cardboard cornflake box and Sellotape.

Anna stands back to let my mother through. I follow. Inside, the rooms are empty. In the living room the chatty furniture has departed, the yellow chair and black chair, the red couch. The bookshelf is gone, and the television, and the mirror and the lamps. In the dining room there is a gaping hole where my grandmother's delicate china cabinet once stood on its claw-shaped tippy-toes. There are indentations on the carpet where the heavy dining-room table used to stand, the table under which I held my important meetings with John.

My mother cries out, short and sharp, like she's been punctured, sliced. Her piano is gone. Its white ghost-shadow, its non-shadow, the shape of its outline, is visible on the empty white wall.

'My piano,' she says. 'My piano.'

The kitchen table is still there, with four chairs around it. Lucky's empty cage is gone, which, to be perfectly honest, is no great loss. Upstairs, they have left us our beds, our blankets, and our clothes, of course, piled up now on the floor, ejected, expelled from their absent wardrobes.

'Did a robber come?' I ask Anna in astonishment.

Anna doesn't want to answer. She has been left here for this very purpose; she has been left here to break the news.

'Couple of days ago,' she says, not looking at my mother, not looking at me. 'They came a couple of days ago. The bailiffs. No one was here. They knocked through the glass on the front door, opened the latch. I came home. I could see them from the top of the road. They were loading up their van.'

I don't know where my father is. I scan the road for sight of him. I don't know what he is driving, or if he is driving. I check the footpath for his long shadow.

My uncle – my mother's brother – and his wife drive over in their Vauxhall car. I'm pleased to see them; they are dignified, reliable, sincere people who subscribe to Reader's Digest and grow gooseberries, and have taken me on caravanning holidays with my cousins, making entirely sure that we all have waterproof jackets and enough knit-wear to last the fortnight. I like them both.

My aunt is a great reader. I look forward to talking to

her about books. While I'm reading, I think about the things I'd like to tell her, things that would interest her.

'What are you reading?' my aunt asks me, settling down at the kitchen table in the midst of the empty echoing chaos. We discuss Noel Streatfeild's clenched life in her father's vicarage, while my mother shows my uncle around our hollow house.

It's a strange feeling, both of us discussing this alternative world, this entirely different reality, as if it's just as interesting and important as what is happening all around us.

It's freeing to divulge the detail, the intricacies, of a life you haven't lived, can never live. To escape into a paper world.

'My piano,' I hear my mother repeat to her brother when she re-encounters its outline on the naked wall. 'My piano.' As if it is all a little preposterous, as if the piano has vanished into thin air and might well reappear in an instant with some fantastic story to recount about its celestial journey.

They come back into the empty kitchen, my uncle shaking his head, sighing, folding his arms, rubbing his jaw. My mother, who can't actually stomach too much calamity at any one time, proposes fish and chips. There is a certain giddiness in the night, a kind of fizzing, like sherbet. It is as if our life is one long dry tongue, sprinkled now with this fizzy strangeness.

We eat the fish and chips at the kitchen table, under the stark fluorescent lightbulb, my mother, Anna, aunt and uncle seated on the remaining chairs. I sit on the edge of the fireplace, my back to the empty hearth.

Anna declines more chips, takes a small mirror out of her jacket pocket and paints on her eyeliner. There is the low growl of a slowing motorbike out on the street. She zips up her skinny leather jacket and goes. I move to take her place at the table.

When I go to bed, I realize that the chaise which used to be under my window, the lying-down couch that came from my grandmother's old house to this new house, this new symmetric house that didn't quite know what to do with it, the chaise that Norah and I used to play 'fainting ladies' on, is gone.

So, too, is my transistor radio.

For a moment, fear obliterates drama, anxiety tops exhilaration. I breathe like Norah has been taught to breathe, head bent forward, hands on my knees, my mouth shaped like a whistle. I breathe: breathing in, breathing out, breathing in, breathing out.

I go back downstairs to see if the kitchen radio is still there, my heart beating fast on the blunt stair carpet. By some miracle, it is still on the windowsill, hiding behind the unyielding curtain, near where Lucky's cage used to be. I take it upstairs, plug it in next to my bed. The late-night disc jockey's voice is a familiar port in this empty ocean.

My father comes home while I am asleep.

The next morning he ties his cravat in the bathroom mirror, which is still conveniently attached to the wall.

'OK, Billy?' he asks, smiling. The small band of sweat over his top lip has returned to greet us like a lost friend.

'Are you OK?' I ask him.

The words I really want to use are 'where is the furniture?' and 'why weren't you here when we came home yesterday?' but those words will just have to find somewhere else to do their talking, because my mouth is playing a blinder.

'Who's Daddy's pal?' he asks. He already knows the answer.

WE DON'T LEAVE OUR ROAD RIGHT AWAY, DON'T IMMEdiately vacate our house. We have a couple of weeks' grace while the bank sells the house and takes back all the money that we should never have spent in the first place.

My mother's friend Cora, the artist, scurries up and down the road with soda bread that she has baked, and scallions that she has grown, and eggs that someone or other's obliging hen has laid. She offers footstools and crochet rugs, anything she can think of, to make our indoor camp more comfortable.

My father flits in and out of the empty house. He looks like Judas the morning after the night before, rattled but unrepentant. My mother, silent and raw as a freshly dug grave, watches him from across the empty kitchen, her back to the lonely cooker.

We stay living in our house long enough for John's postcard to arrive. He is in Portugal, preparing to depart for the Azores. From there, he will sail on to the Caribbean, then maybe on across the Atlantic to America. He's heard that someone is looking for crew to deliver a boat to Africa. Africa. Africa feels farther away than the moon, the moon at least being visible through a stripped-clean bedroom window.

John has heard the news of our forthcoming departure. Our casting off. He will use Louise's new address for future postcards, he says. Who knows where we'll be? Who knows where he'll be?

My father disappears again for two days and a night. My mother and I, with an ear out for the sound of his key in the latch, make a bonfire in the long back garden. We burn all the old returned cheques in the black sack that has been clogging up her wardrobe floor. We burn Louise's and Anna's and John's barely scratched schoolbooks. We burn unkind letters from the bank. We burn scrapbooks filled with recipes, cut out and glued in over the years: beef stroganoff, chicken à la king, tunnel of fudge. We burn paper patterns for peasant blouses and boleros and dirndl skirts, and one for a child's full-length nightie. The dressmaking patterns have been cut out and pinned to fabric, flimsy crinkled paper laid down and chalked on to remnants, fitted ingeniously on to paisley-print oddments from bargain baskets; patterns that have been followed, realized, refolded and carefully replaced in their illustrated envelopes. We don't need them any more. The sewing machine is gone too.

When our small fire is burnt out, there is a scorched yellow ring on the grass, and slivers of silvery-grey paper floating around like leaves from a moon tree.

I am upstairs when I hear his key in the door. My mother hears it too. She flies out of the kitchen, comes to a stop in the narrow hall. I assume my position on the stairway, behind the ironwork, to watch his prodigal return.

'What happened?' she asks.

'Nothing. Nothing. I got nothing. I hitch-hiked home from Galway. Couldn't make the price of the train.'

He is wearing his father's beautiful old grey tweed coat, flecked with red and blue and yellow. It's hot outside. It probably wasn't hot when he left his sister's hotel in the west of Ireland, empty-handed, and put his thumb out and began his journey home.

Something happens that I have never seen before. His head falls forward, in defeat, in exhaustion maybe. My mother walks towards him. One tiny step, one giant leap. She reaches him. She puts her arms around him. She holds him. His head rests on her shoulder; his face is a plate of tears.

I feel stupefied. I feel full of confusion and rage and turmoil and a terrible boiling anger that has nowhere to go but back inside the pocket of my shorts. I move silently upstairs to my empty bedroom, stare at the empty walls. Who are those strangers embracing in our hallway? Why have they forgotten their lines all of a sudden? Since when did they become characters in this other, sentimental, play, this pantomime of love and loss and forgiveness? This unsettling piece of theatre that no one wants to watch? Why don't they just get on with the performance we are all comfortably familiar with, the Punch and Judy show they've been peddling since they met?

I have never seen them touch each other before. I am shaking.

His trip to the west of Ireland was, apparently, to try to secure somewhere for us to live. There were other possibilities that his sister may have been able to realize, a house on the other side of the bay that we might have been able to rent. But it wasn't to be. No blame. No re-crimination. After all, nobody's life is as fortunate as it may appear.

Anna is packing up her clothes. She has filled half a dozen bin bags already, and there are still belts sneaking around the bed legs, bandannas and bracelets multiplying underneath the mattress. When she is finished, she sits on the carpet next to her bed, pushes her blue-black hair behind her ears. She looks at me for a minute, like she's just realized I'm there. Visible or not, I'm doing remarkably well out of Anna's over-capacity on the bin-bag front. She's bequeathed me three cheesecloth shirts, one of them cerulean blue with yellow embroidery around the neck.

'You'll grow into them, I suppose,' she says. Her breath catches. She lights a cigarette.

Anna is ferocious, but only like a puppy is ferocious if you try to pull its blanket away and it holds on with its milk teeth, snarling and growling, like a grown-up dog. Anna is generous; she leaves her tips around in a jar in case we run out of things.

Anna plans to stay with Louise until she can find a bedsit near the city. Her hours in the salon are long. She has clients with knotty pink Afros, and poker-straight blondes, and any number of other dead-cool people with big ideas about their barnets, all demanding her time in the famously funky unisex salon where she has started to work.

I don't think she wants to live in a bedsit, even if it is really cool and she can hang Aubrey Beardsley posters on the wall and throw a tie-dyed cotton scarf over the lampshade to make everything look mystical and far out.

She stands up when she hears the engine slow. Anna and her bearded boyfriend pile the bags into the back seat of his borrowed car, his motorbike being inadequate for the occasion.

Louise calls over later to collect her painted stones, which she never did manage to sell in the end. She has her own small garden to decorate now, her own back door to prop open with rocks the size and smoothness of ostrich eggs.

It is so hard to tell if Louise is happy or sad. She looks wistful, tentative; she looks like she is trying to catch a moth that keeps crashing into the light, and eludes and eludes her. Louise is the fairest of them all. Not that she is blonde; her hair is autumn-coloured. She is the fairest in the fairy-book sense, in the sleep-for-one-hundred-years-in-a-glass-coffin-and-wake-up-hoping-things-might-have-moved-on-a-bit sense.

Spent matches in their bedroom hearth, hair-clips on their mantelpiece, the gold buckle from Anna's turquoise hot pants glowing under her abandoned bed. The bullet hole in their window pane. The pebble wound, the gunshot crack, still there, untrammelled, outlined still in pillar-box-red nail varnish.

Kapow. They've gone. My sisters have gone.

My brother's room is empty too. One loose Styrofoam ceiling tile tries to break away from the rest. Got to hand it to the old bailiffs, they certainly don't leave much of a mess. Like locusts, they strip a place clean.

Kapow. Sisters gone. Brother gone.

'Louise is gone,' I tell my mother. 'Anna is gone. John is gone.'

'I know,' she says, blowing smoke at the moon. 'I know.'

We borrow my brother-in-law's Morris Traveller, pack it up with our sheets and towels, with our winter clothes and summer clothes.

My grey school uniform is on a hanger on the back seat; my mouse suit, my convent costume. The sleeve of the jumper, rising in a gust of air from the open door, beckons me, calls me over. It wants to whisper in my ear, tell me what is about to befall us, my cuff-chewed jumper and I. I didn't know then, or maybe I did; maybe I always knew how the final dance with Sister Immaculate would play.

I wouldn't need my mouse suit for very much longer. Just long enough to wind my way back to school in September. Long enough to find Norah, breathing steady, for now, eyes gleaming with wild plans after her long, still hospitalization. Long enough to slip into our shared wooden desk and whisper the news of our departure from the neighbourhood.

'We'll go to America,' Norah says. 'We'll ride a Greyhound bus, look out the window at the great big cowboy landscape; we'll eat pancakes and maple syrup, and then we'll ride the bus back home again.'

'We're not even eleven,' I remind her. 'We're not eleven yet.'

I need my uniform just long enough for Sister Immaculate to call me into her office, where I find my mother waiting, tight-lipped, bathed in fury, while Sister Immaculate instructs her to take me home.

I'm to be expelled. I'm weak. Weak, weak, weak. I don't belong in this world of polished parquet and pristine plinths. My mother has been instructed to take me home, to find somewhere more suitable for me to continue my education, a national school maybe.

'You may collect your shoe bag on the way out,' she says to me. 'You won't be needing it any more.'

Her lips are so still, her smile so fixed and flat, I wonder if there is a ventriloquist in the room.

'She's done nothing wrong,' my mother says, her hands shaking with anger. 'She's a child. She's done nothing wrong.'

'Indeed,' says smiling Sister Immaculate. 'Indeed.'

And so we pack our sheets and towels, our summer clothes and winter clothes. We pack up the car with our pots and pans, with cups and saucers and knives and forks, with the ornaments that have survived the purge: china poodles in little china sweaters, a wooden napkin ring, three brass napkin rings, a cut-glass candle holder that skidded one Christmas night to the floor and was amazed at its own survival. We take our books and drawings and photographs, and my mother's sheet music, which has decided to accompany us even though the piano never did return to earth.

I'm being dropped off at Dawn's house for a week or two, while my parents sort out a place for us to live.

'Will I have to eat tongue?' I ask my father.

'Probably. Probably best to eat it before it eats you.'

Dawn and I will play Happy Families on the floor next to her big, boxy colour television set. Mr and Mrs Bun, the bakers, with their great big doughy daughter and hot cross son; Mr and Mrs Green, the gardeners, with their muddy son and willowy daughter.

We will sit next to the little tree that pushes up through her living-room floor, the little sapling that refuses to be uprooted, that insists on its right to push through the foundations and reach up to the light.

'Whadda you waaant me to do?' asks Dawn's mother. 'It's a tree. Trees are cute.'

When the car is bursting at the back-door seams, we go back inside for one final look.

Carpet. Bulb. Tile. Nothing.

The bank has sold the house to some man who turned up in the empty kitchen one evening in a trilby. Snapped it up.

'For a song,' my mother laments.

The car is ticking over. My mother lingers on the porch, where the caravan woman used to sit, waiting patiently, biding her time, taking the weight off her bare, broken-veined legs. 'Join me in a cup, ma'am, and I'll read the leaves for you. What harm could it do you, ma'am?'

No harm at all, because what happens happens, and what doesn't happen doesn't happen, and we're really none the wiser anyway.

My friends from the road stand around our gate in an uneasy circle, scuffing the backs of their worn summer sandals against the pebbledash garden wall. None of us much more than a decade old, we have never really had recourse to say goodbye to anything, or anybody, bar the occasional dead budgerigar or a hamster missing in action because someone forgot to close its cage.

'Right?' says my father from the driver's seat.

'I'll see ya,' I say to the sandal-wearers.

'See ya,' they say back.

None of us move.

'Okay?' enquires my father through the open passenger door. 'Billy?'

The smiling neighbour hugs my mother over the garden wall. Baby girls, toddler girls, girl girls nod and wave and bounce.

'Right,' he says again. 'We go, yeah? We get going, all right?'

My mother sits into the car, checks her reflection in the rear-view mirror.

He turns the key.

There is a moment of stillness, a moment of silence, a moment frozen, an inconsequential moment like when a glass breaks, a fast scattering of everything that it used to be. Shards on the kitchen floor. 'Oh, it's nothing,' someone says. 'Just a glass. I'll get the dustpan and brush.'

The ignition catches.

We drive down the road away from the estate, swing left out on to the coast, follow its outline towards the isthmus, follow the scent of the sea and the call of the gulls.

'It's an adventure,' my father tells me from the driver's seat, his eyes catching mine in the readjusted mirror. 'It's an adventure. We'll get a dog.'

'What kind of dog?'

'You say. What kind of dog do you want?'

'I don't want a dog,' says my mother. 'Christ on a

fucking stick! We don't have a home; what are we going to do with a dog?'

'What kind of dog?' he asks again.

'A black dog. A black dog with brown eyes. And teeth.'

'And teeth,' he repeats. 'Okay, a black dog it is. A black dog, with teeth, it is.'

Home

MY FATHER DIED IN THE YEAR 2000, IN MID-December. Finally, after a comatose week in his hospital bed, he slipped anchor and set out on his dark voyage, a week before Christmas, on a cold, navy-blue night.

We had watched, over the course of that wintery week, his lips blacken and his skin yellow, watched him sink under the crib of his ribcage as if his body was exhaling itself in one long ragged sigh.

There was relief in his departure, relief when he slipped beyond our reach. His illness, played out in uneven bursts of enthusiasm and remission, had dogged him for almost five years. Cancer.

He died late at night, at ten to one in the morning.

At ten to one in the morning, a metal bucket outside Anna's back door blew over in a sudden flurry of wind, and somewhere a dog howled, plaintive and sharp, into the ice-still night.

'He's gone,' my mother said, and then the telephone rang.

We were all sitting around Anna's kitchen table, eating Irish stew and drinking wine. My mother, who, in her early seventies, still wouldn't put the bins out without her lipstick on, was enjoying the company but wary of what the new dispensation would bring.

His death would soon precipitate a move out of the elegantly located small, damp flat she and he had rented for the last number of years, the flat they had lived in ever since they had moved out of the equally damp quixotic little house, right next door, which they had rented for years and years before that.

In the years since they had dropped me off to stay at Dawn's house to play Happy Families and gag on tongue, while they went off in search of a rent they could afford, they, and I, had lived in four different dwellings, each within a narrow radius, each within sight of the sea. All the houses were small and dramatically situated, all slightly mad and damp; all boasted oddly combined furnishings, cast-offs, usually, of the various landlords who owned the properties. My mother spent years decorating blistered chairs with throws and cushions, years hand-painting old cupboards with hearts and flowers. The kitchen of the crooked house they stayed in the longest ended up looking, not entirely unattractively, like the set of an amateur pantomime.

'Will we be dining with the elves tonight?' my father would enquire, pulling up a chair decorated with painted daisies and a brave attempt at lupins.

The threat of découpage followed us from house to house, from one tired surface to the next. My mother's desire to cover anything that stayed still long enough with

219

seashells also meant we were awash with wine-bottle lamp bases, covered in Polyfilla and crustaceans. I remember a book that travelled with us from house to house: *One Hundred Plus Ideas for Polyfilla*. A title that held not a hint of irony.

I still can't pass a scallop shell without picturing a crushed-out cigarette in its base, the tip rimmed in pearly pink lipstick.

For the most part, the houses we rented were lonely, isolated, crouching at the ends of lanes or muddy tracks. And although we no longer had neighbours, or certainly none that I could play with, no one who would knock on your front door with a doll's pram and three Ginger Nut biscuits, the properties generally came with an assortment of wildlife – dogs and cats, and unwelcome mice, an occasional hedgehog, an intermittent badger – blocking the path to the front door.

The first house they rented was perched on the side of a cliff, illuminated by night, with metronomic precision, by the lighthouse on the opposite cove. The windows, a big sea visible through every one, had to be washed clean of sea salt after the frequent storms. It was a narrow, cold house, with a mosaic-covered larder built into the outside wall. A long wooden spine-like corridor gripped the house, pulled it towards the hewn-out cliff face, stopped it from tumbling down into the waves.

The brown-eyed black dog, with the razor-sharp teeth, who materialized shortly after we moved in, and who lived for a couple of wild, untrammelled years with us (until he ended up under the little red bus that traversed the neighbourhood), used to pound up and down the long corridor on his coltish paws, leaping into the air on his last stride and landing on top of my father in his slim bed at the end of the house.

The loss of the family home never seemed to discourage my father. If anything, being untethered from the suburban street, being free of the banks, being cast aside by more conventional fields of employment, he seemed released. He was happier; he started cartooning. Work, if not particularly remunerative, was regular. The rent got paid.

My mother too, faced with the reality of their situation, understanding the precarious nature of their lives, looked for a way to make a living. She found employment with the order of nuns whom her sister had joined all those auburn-haired years before. She began teaching drama, to little girls in big school uniforms, in various of the order's convent schools, bussing around the city suburbs with her drama books and her lipstick and her packed lunch in her basket.

It would be untrue to say that pain ceased, that rows were silenced, that recriminations were spirited away with the sea mist. There were long nights when the dog and I would lie, looking at each other, in my small, partitioned bedroom, listening to the roll and crash of their regret.

We had a working telephone again. One Saturday morning, shortly after the dog had found an eviscerated water rat to roll in and was eluding a dousing with a bucket of water by running around and around the perimeter of the house, me running around and around after it, the water steadily decreasing in volume, the telephone rang.

'Shoot him if you want,' I heard my mother say to the

caller. 'Come down with the gun, be my guest, you know where we are. I don't mind. Really. But think what it will do to Billy.'

The caller apologized. He never did come with his gun, Snowdrift's husband. He was far too nice a man.

I never saw Snowdrift again. I picked up rumours, stray talk, snippets of information discarded like litter, that I poked through, looking for clues.

She may have become ill. The illness, whatever it was, remained unspecific. Some walls of silence are difficult to climb. The big house, the portal to heaven that he and I visited, where her invisible presence was so visible, was sold.

Snow melts, I suppose.

After two, maybe three, years, my parents' cliffside house was sold too. For a song they couldn't afford to sing. We moved.

MY FATHER DIED AT TEN TO ONE IN THE MORNING.

At ten to one in the morning, a metal bucket outside Anna's back door blew over, her husband stood to look outside, disturbing a lone dog patrolling the sleeping suburb. The dog howled, plaintive and sharp, into the ice-still night.

'He's gone,' my mother said, and then the telephone rang.

Sitting next to my mother that night at Anna's table was my brother John, home from Bristol, where he lived with his family. No more than my mother's, John's life was about to change too. More than thirty years after his education had been amputated, at the age of fifteen, he was about to go to university in his adopted city. A diagnosis of dyslexia in his fifties, and the supports that the university offered, would see him complete a degree and a master's, and write and publish two novels in the space of four years. It would also see him return to the same college, just months after his graduation, to take up a teaching post in the English department there.

John had spent years working in the Caribbean, skippering boats. And years ashore, writing, drawing, sign-writing, painting and decorating; turning a buck. He and my father had finally sailed together, both of them crew on a small yacht that headed out of the harbour and up into the Arctic ice. They'd negotiated their own truce, on long night watches together, phosphorescence bouncing off the water, and in Reykjavik discotheques, and in a capsize in a freezing sea, after which the crew lay on the deck in a pyramid shape to keep hypothermia at bay with body warmth, my father, the eldest aboard, lying at the base with a man either side.

Next to John that night at Anna's was Louise, generous, distracted, delicate. She had survived cancer in her thirties and was, unknown to all of us, heading into a second skirmish with the disease, one which she would also endure and outlast. A mother to two adult children, she taught painting now. Empathetic, unassuming, her classes were often given in therapeutic environments. Louise, with her disarming mixture of practicality and eccentricity, had that afternoon opened all the windows in my father's hospital room and asked the nurses to moisten his mouth with a lemon-flavoured stick, this man who, for whatever reason, could not bring himself to visit her when she herself had lain, bird-like, in her own hospital bed.

Next to Louise was her husband, generously not drinking in case anyone needed a lift anywhere.

'What is the difference between Protestants and Catholics?' we asked him, drink flowing into our own glasses.

'Gravy,' he replied. 'Protestants prefer theirs runny.'

The metal bucket outside Anna's back door blew over. The dog howled.

'He's gone,' my mother said. The telephone rang. Anna stood to answer it.

Some of us journeyed in the soberly driven car, the rest of us took a taxi.

Earlier on that shallow, silvery day, while Christmas shoppers boarded buses clutching their lists and schoolchildren glued on wings and fleeces and moustaches for their Nativity plays, Anna and I had walked through the park, the park whose treetops were just visible from the window of our father's hospital room. We walked carefully down the narrow, ice-dazzled paths, our hands deep in our pockets. I was stiff from sitting all night in the hospital chair beside his bed.

At dawn, when the nurses had come in to turn him, I had gone outside into the corridor, stretched, jumped up and down, shaken my head from side to side like a bit-snapping pony.

I could hear the animal moan as they lifted him to lie

him on his other side, a low primitive howl of indignation. He was just muffled pain now, it seemed to me; muted pain and drugs, discomfort and drip-fed relief, and breath so slow to reach the surface that it could have been drawn from a well.

The night nurse popped her head out of the ward kitchen, waved a pack of cigarettes at me. We headed out on to the fire escape, made sharp exhalations into the dawn.

'How long has he got left, do you think?' I asked the nurse.

'Not long now, hopefully, not too much longer,' she said.

We left the fire escape, her for her bed, me to tether myself to my father's for another hour or so.

When John arrived he told me that Anna was waiting downstairs for me, beside the life-sized statue of the Sacred Heart, the great big plaster effigy that dominated the hospital foyer.

'She says you're to go for a walk. You'll need air.'

My whole fucking family are obsessed with air, I thought, as I walked down the curved staircase to meet her.

When we had brought my father here, a fortnight or so before, he had stopped to gaze at that statue of the Sacred Heart, its beating red core lit up from within like a huge Christmas bauble. I had stood next to him holding his sailing bag, packed with his dressing gown and slippers and the new lilac-coloured pyjamas that I had bought for him in a moment of unwarranted optimism.

'That poor fucker only came in to have his appendix out,' he said, looking up at the benign plaster Jesus.

We moved slowly to the lift.

*

'I spoke to the night nurse this morning,' I told Anna as we walked through the winter park. 'She doesn't think it will be long now. Not too much longer now, she thinks.'

'I'll take the Irish stew out of the freezer,' Anna replied.

THERE HAD BEEN TALK IN THE DAYS RUNNING UP TO this – his comatose state, his last kingdom before death – of some class of intervention; talk, while he was still in the shared ward, distressed and yellowing in the lilac pyjamas, about removing the cancerous tumour from his liver. Stray, alarming ideas were whispered around his bed about some kind of surgical resurrection. I was dismayed. I couldn't imagine a single good reason why.

Anna and I had walked the same paths then, past the same obsequiously weeping willow, to discuss his possible return to earth.

'What? What are they talking about? He's dying,' said Anna.

'There's talk about operating, then maybe sending him somewhere to dry out, to see if they can get him another year or two.'

'He'd hate to dry out. A year or two to do what? Live how? For Christ's sake.'

'Maybe they think we'll sue. Some people want to hang on to every last drop.'

'Every last drop of what? He'd rather shoot himself than wake up in some drying-out unit. He wouldn't be able to shoot himself; he wouldn't have the wherewithal. Some-

226

body else would have to do it for him. You. You'd have to shoot him. You're his favourite.'

'Thanks,' I replied.

'The man is dying. And anyway, I've already put an Irish stew in the freezer for when he goes.'

Anna is a cook. After cutting hair for thirty years, she just stopped. Threw down her scissors, opened a recipe book, and the rest followed.

Christmases, birthdays, hangovers, bitter regrets, have all played out across Anna's kitchen table. Anna, who could scald you with a look, slice through you with a flick of her freshly ironed jet-black hair, could disappear you with the sharp exhale of her cigarette smoke. Anna provides.

She watched her fourteen-year-old daughter playing on a swing one day, she told me. Standing at her kitchen sink, looking out into the green behind her house, she saw Kate, laughing, turn upside down on a tree swing. Anna's hands stilled in the soapy water. She's a child, Anna thought, she's just a little girl playing on a swing. And Anna felt a great wave of sadness for the little girl that she was at fourteen, bussing it into town to sweep up hair eight hours a day; for all the children working eight-hour days when they should have been on a tree swing.

'We'll talk to the consultant,' Anna said. 'Go home. John and I will talk to him.'

'You have to go to the ethics committee. They need to know that we all feel the same way.'

'We do feel the same way.'

'Maybe they think we're too unsentimental, too blunt.'

'All right, we're not the shagging Waltons, but, Christ, they can't do that to him.'

Trudging back up the icy path, I wondered if the doctors had noticed what Louise and John had done to the surgical gloves.

During that long week there were various meetings with the team. I tried to listen to the surgeon as he enumerated the possible reasons for intervening in my father's limited future. I tried to stop my mind from wandering.

I thought about him, on cold mornings, in the tiny kitchen of the flat he shared with my mother, warming whiskey in the base of his porridge bowl. I thought about him pleading with the morning news to say something funny or absurd that he could use for his daily box cartoon in the evening paper. I thought of him coming home late in the evening and sitting in the main room of that almost hidden flat, looking out at the summer rain pouring down on the jungle-like garden beyond the shuttered window frames, looking up at the big wet sky above the eucalyptus trees, a wine bottle by his side, a plastic bucket on the table to catch the drips from the leaking ceiling.

'Look at the moon,' he'd command anyone who might be listening, usually the indifferent cat. 'Look at the moon, look at the moon, look at the pale-green moon.'

('Surgery alone won't guarantee . . .' the consultant continued.)

I thought of him in the dark bar he frequented at lunchtime, after drawing that morning, at a shared desk under a narrow stairwell, in an office on a Georgian square.

I thought of his friends, his amiable cohort – the poet, the ad man, the sailor, the hack – whom he met daily for convivial glasses of purple wine and a beef-and-onion sandwich. He hadn't had a bank account for years; if someone paid him with a cheque, he simply handed it to the barman.

'I don't know why anyone needs banks when there are bars,' he said to me one day. We were on Baggot Street in Dublin city. I was carrying my infant son, in a sling on my front, to the car, parked on the other side of the square. My father was walking behind me, leaning heavily on both my shoulders, the pain in his gut so great he could barely take each laboured step. We progressed like a decommissioned train, suited commuters whizzing past us on the crowded pavement.

How will I get him home? I wondered to myself. How in the name of God will I get him home?

'We'll garotte that mushrooming growth, lacerate the malignant spores. Our job, after all, is to keep him alive so that death can find him.'

'I'm sorry,' I said to the surgeon. 'I wasn't listening. You were saying?'

'I was saying that surgery alone won't necessarily guarantee . . .'

I tried to imagine my father drying out, waking up to a world of cups of tea and an evening paper and naps in front of the nine o'clock news; a world of garden centres and hanging baskets and begonias. I tried to imagine his survival in a technological world.

'What in the name of Christ is a fax machine?' he had

roared when someone had suggested he might use one to file his cartoons. 'How can I feed my drawings into a fucking telephone?'

He had heard the beast of a new modernity sing. He didn't want to look beyond the sedative gloom of a lunchtime barroom, to face a screen-glow future.

'Let him go,' I wanted to say to the cautious surgeon, but I didn't know how.

I was tired. I wanted to go home to my small son in my two-up-two-down city home.

As the man spoke, I imagined surgeons in spats, sharpening their scalpels on kidney stones. 'We will keep him alive,' they sang. 'Alive-alive-oh, alive-alive-oh. We'll sluice out his bones, hang them in a stiff breeze. We'll polish his brasses and iron his pyjamas and stand him upright at a locked window, in a shaft of evening sun, to wave goodbye to a departing family saloon.

'He'll soon forget about his snooker games, his pints lined up along the shuttered bar. He'll just have to pull up his bargain-basement Argyle socks,' sang the physicians.

'This is a new country now, don't you know?' they crooned, lassoing a gaggle of cats with their stethoscopes. 'We're not some milk-stained backwater, where deals are done and cheques are cashed in genial bars over pints of porter. Sober and straight and stitched and sutured, that's the way we want him. Then he can go home and sit in a chair, and have a biscuit, and wait to die, abstemiously, moderately, properly, of stone-cold old age.'

'I'm sorry,' I said to the patient surgeon. 'What were you saying?'

'Go home,' said the doctor. 'Think about what I've said.'

*

My father's leave-taking hadn't been altogether bleak. There were convivial times in that crisp white December-lit hospital room when friends gathered to say goodbye. Some stood around his bed, arms folded, heads thrown back, talking about rugby and President Clinton's state visit, the boyo, their eyes reluctantly glancing off my father's shallowly breathing frame. Other friends, his artier, ratty-sleeved cohorts, turned up to bid a slower farewell to the waxen figure in their midst.

There were times in that bite-cold, empty-skied December week, in the small orbit of that place, while the rest of the city was rushing around buying the last of the Cheeky Charlies and bottles of sweet perfume, that his hospital room was almost festive, ringing with conversation and the low rumble of reminiscences.

It sounded, from outside on the sterile corridor, as if you might push open the door and find a bar, a gin on a wooden countertop, a pint settling in a glass.

We were tough, his children, the uneven chorus behind his life, unsentimental deckhands watching the deepening water while he navigated the course to death.

On one shared shift, Louise and John blew up half a dozen surgical gloves, drew faces with black marker on the fattened palms and tied them to his bedhead, the aerated fingers standing up like spiked, electrified hair.

The little Latex rubber souls, sentinels, floated above him, smiling, bobbing from side to side, looking out for death's arrival like enthusiastic children at a country station waiting for someone extraordinary to alight from a train.

IT TOOK VERY LITTLE IN THE END FOR THE ETHICS COM-mittee to be persuaded that intervention was probably not a good idea, and to let death take her course. And take her course she did, slowly, meandering along the byways of his faded musculature, roving around the back alleys of his sunken veins, meeting the subcutaneous fluids that were keeping his leathery body hydrated, hiding in the shadow of his eyes.

At one stage in the intervening days, John and I met in a nearby bar to compose the death notice. We sat up at the quiet bar, among escapees from the season. John ordered a pint for himself, a gin for me. I took out my notebook to write down suitable adjectives.

'He died . . . tragically?'

'Fuck no.'

'Peacefully?'

'You joking me?'

'Suddenly?'

'Hardly.'

'Eventually?' I suggested.

'Write that down.'

('We will not say that he died eventually,' said my mother later, in a rush of irritation.

'He was a cartoonist, he'd think it was funny.'

'We will not say that he died eventually,' said my mother again, 'we will say he died peacefully. Whether he does or not.')

We sat in the friendly yellow-smoke bar. My resolution to give the damn things up was going precisely nowhere.

'I was leaving his room last night when the nun came in. She sits with him in the night if he's alone. She's good, compassionate. She talks to him. She says he can hear, she says he can understand.

'I told her that he believed in nothing, that nothing she could say would comfort him. He didn't believe in gods, or druids, or numbs. He'd sooner put his faith in the deification of domestic cats.

'She said: "In my father's house there are many mansions." For a moment I actually believed her.

'When I was driving home, I started thinking about Norah. I'd wanted to read a poem at her funeral, an Emily Dickinson poem. Bleak, sober, human. I was young. I don't know why I didn't. Someone handed me a bidding prayer, something about thanking God for letting us know her, during her short sojourn on earth. I read it, I was grateful to be asked. I thought, but what about the life she won't live, what about the person we won't know? I didn't feel the presence of any God.'

John gestured for another round.

'She'd returned home from America, she'd written it all down, in a journal, her travels across that continent, on the Greyhound buses, sleeping in shelters, talking to people, she was so alive. She just ran out of breath.'

'Do you remember that bar in Rhode Island?' John asked, watching his pint settle on the bar. 'You were skint, I was skint, we were drinking dollar-a-shot Kamikazes and Destroyers? Remember? And it was nearly like we evoked him, do you remember? As if memory could conjure someone up.'

I remembered.

233

We were sitting in that bar in Rhode Island, in the afternoon, drinking cheap shots. Down on the wharf, preppy young Americans in dusty-pink polo shirts were stretching their suntanned legs out along the jetty, sipping ten-dollar Margaritas and enjoying the ocean view. Broke, we wouldn't be joining them.

At nearly twenty years of age, I'd finally succeeded in leaving Ireland. I'd got a job in Connecticut at a summer camp, where the days were punctuated by the canteen bell ringing out under big passive skies, blue and cloudless and effortless, scorched by darting red cardinals.

It was 1981. There were no jobs back home. I'd queued up for hours along a sticky stair carpet in a Dublin hotel to find summer work in America. We stood in line – students, the unemployed – all the way up the stairs, from shabby lobby to stuffy interview room, without a shard of orthodontistry between us.

Out of school for a couple of years, my employment skills were limited, though waitressing had suited me fine until I convinced myself that polishing cutlery and recommending the Hawaiian burger was an unambitious career choice. I had worked then in care jobs in a couple of bleak residential homes for children. I was unhappy, but no more unhappy than anyone else I was acquainted with at the time. It just felt like the world moved on in its mysterious directions while I stood still, that's all. Sometimes, passing Trinity College on my way to a shift, I watched skinny boys in army-surplus coats walking under the archway, rolled-up cigarettes between their lips, scarves hanging around their necks like lists of obscure intentions. I watched girls with scraped-back hair, and bags the size of small children hanging from their shoulders, disappear with their bicycles underneath that archway into a medieval gloom on the other side. They were another breed. Students. Rarer than buses.

I got the summer job in America. My remuneration for six weeks' work was the price of my airline ticket. The summer camp was for children with physical and intellectual needs. I was an old hand.

My boyfriend gave me a card with a picture of Uncle Sam on the front and a one-hundred-dollar bill inside. 'A Buck for Every Fuck,' he wrote, in his austere calligraphy.

It was my first time on an aeroplane.

In America, I was ambushed by the steam ballooning out of the subways and amazed by the quilted bathroom tissue. I met a Jewish boy from Brooklyn who brought me to the New York planetarium on our day off, and, as Jupiter birthed her litter of Galilean moons, wiped his glasses on his shirtsleeves and asked me home for dinner. His mother collected figurines from *Fiddler on the Roof.* I thought I was in a movie.

When the six weeks of work on the summer camp were up, and I was brown and lonely and vaguely fat from the endlessly ringing food bell, I took the remains of my hundred-dollar bill and bussed my way to Newport, in Rhode Island, to find John. He'd recently arrived from the Caribbean on a sailing boat he'd delivered. He was living aboard, on rye bread and Spam, waiting for the owner to turn up and pay him.

And so we sat, in the afternoon gloom, my brother

and I, looking into our oily shot glasses, in the only bar in Rhode Island that didn't have a bell jar of cinnamon muffins on the countertop and a hospitality enthusiast urging us to have a nice day every time we ordered a refill. Nobody in that dark bar was going to be having a nice day, today, tomorrow or any time soon.

I was overwhelmingly glad to see him.

'Ahem, ahem.' We cleared our throats. We were very good mimics; we knew this game. We threw the paraffin-scented shots down our throat. One after the other after the other. I concentrated on keeping my elbow on the countertop; it wanted to fold up like an occasional table, reappear for a more salubrious occasion.

'Christ on a fucking stick,' we said. 'Christ. On. A. Fucking. Stick.'

We winced. We were Oscar-winning wincers. We cleared our throats. We sighed tediously. Spoke quietly. Gave each syllable space to breathe, each word enough rope to hang itself. We were such very good mimics. We could create our father out of a torn-up beer mat, we could invoke him with our voices in this smoky American air.

'You are a wart on my palm,' my brother said.

'You. Are. A. Wart. On. My. Palm,' I repeated.

'Remove it,' he said, flicking the imaginary excrescence at the rat-beard barman.

'Remove it,' I echoed back.

We sounded so like him we startled ourselves. We turned towards the open door, almost as if we were expecting him to be standing there. Sunlight shouldered up against the jamb, trying to get inside. He wasn't. Why would he be?

'They bought a washing machine,' I told my brother, empty shot glasses surrounding us like a posse. 'An automatic washing machine. Their first. You can see the clothes going around and around, through the fish eye in the door.'

'Yeah?'

I told my brother about the night the machine was delivered to the pantomime kitchen. How my father had pulled a chair up and sat in front of it, a glass of wine in his hand, the big, white, rat-catching cat on his knee, a willing audience, waiting for the domestic cabaret to begin. And in that kitchen, where they lived in their brokered peace, their eroded war, the machine cleared its gurgling pipes and began its concert, its wash, rinse and drain, and my father sat, for the entire cycle, happily saluting his acrobatic Y-fronts every time they did a twirl.

Two more dollars, two more shots.

'You could miss the fucker.'

'You could,' I replied. 'I suppose you could.'

Acknowledgements

First, I'd like to acknowledge the spirited generosity of my family towards this book: my mother, Marie Fannin, my sisters Laura (Louise) and Valerie (Anna), my brother Robert (John) and my brother-in-law Ian Averill.

Huge thanks go to my agent Sharon Bowers, to publisher Eoin McHugh and to my wonderful editor Brian Langan; to copy-editor Anne O'Brien; to Sarah Whittaker for her beautiful cover; and to all at Transworld.

To the many encouraging voices over the years, thank you. I'm particularly grateful to Michèle Forbes and Maureen White, but most especially to my husband, Giles Newington. I've plundered his editorial talents for years and years and years now.

And finally my heartfelt thanks to my old friend Karen Courtney and to the family of Norah Brennan. I hope in some small way that Norah lives on these pages.

Hilary Fannin
Dublin, 2015

Hilary Fannin is a playwright and columnist. Her plays, including *Mackerel Sky*, *Doldrum Bay*, *Famished Castle* and an adaptation of Racine's *Phaedra*, have been performed in Ireland, London, Europe and America. She was writer in association at the Abbey Theatre in its centenary year, 2004. She has also written extensively for radio, both for BBC and RTÉ.

As a journalist, she wrote the TV review for *The Irish Times* for almost five years, passing on the baton when her eyes turned square. She now writes a weekly column for the paper.

Hilary lives in Dublin with her husband and two sons, Peter and Jake. *Hopscotch* is her first full-length prose work.